RISING

FEARLESS WOMEN REBELLING

BY
ROBYN WILLIAMS

RISING:

FEARLESS WOMEN REBELLING

Copyright © 2024 by Robyn Williams

All rights reserved. No part of this publication may be reproduced, stored in a retrieval system, or transmitted in any form or by any means, electronic, mechanical, photocopying, recording, or otherwise, without written permission of the publisher or author, except for the use of brief quotations in a book review.

Although the author and publisher have made every effort to ensure that the information in this book was correct at press time, the author and publisher do not assume and hereby disclaim any liability to any party for any loss, damage, or disruption caused by errors or omissions, whether such errors or omissions result from negligence, accident, or any other cause.

Adherence to all applicable laws and regulations, including international, federal, state and local governing professional licensing, business practices, advertising, and all other aspects of doing business in the US, Canada or any other jurisdiction is the sole responsibility of the reader and consumer.

Neither the author nor the publisher assumes any responsibility or liability whatsoever on behalf of the consumer or reader of this material. Any perceived slight of any individual or organization is purely unintentional.

The resources in this book are provided for informational purposes only and should not be used to replace the specialized training and professional judgment of a health care or mental health care professional.

Neither the author nor the publisher can be held responsible for the use of the information provided within this book. Please always consult a trained professional before making any decision regarding treatment of yourself or others.

To request permissions, contact the publisher at publish@joapublishing.com

Hardcover ISBN: 978-1-961098-67-1
Paperback ISBN: 978-1-961098-66-4
eBook ISBN: 978-1-961098-68-8
Printed in the USA.

Joan of Arc Publishing
Meridian, ID 83646
www.joapublishing.com

TABLE OF CONTENTS

Introduction 1

Trigger Warning 5

Prelude 7

Chapter 1: A Grove, but Make It Pleasant 11

Chapter 2: The Trail of Discernment 16

Chapter 3: Goodbye to My Former Self 33

Chapter 4: One Life Saved, Now Millions 41

Chapter 5: Fear Isn't the Liar . . . You Are 53

Chapter 6: Stage Four Fawner 63

Chapter 7: The Chalk Line in the Dirt 77

Chapter 8: Accountability Is Our Responsibility 87

Chapter 9: Breaking Free 96

Chapter 10: Better than Nothing 105

Chapter 11: The Chains Were Never Locked 110

Chapter 12: Rage Is the Catalyst 116

Chapter 13: You Can Figure it Out.. 123

Chapter 14: The Broken Pieces.. 130

Chapter 15: Self-Love... 133

Chapter 16: The Invitation... 142

Chapter 17: Intuition 149

Chapter 18: Trust 154

Chapter 19: Challenging Beliefs 165

Chapter 20: Revised Narrative... 173

Chapter 21: The Death of the Pleaser 178

Chapter 22: The Grief of the Lost Dream 181

Chapter 23: From Victim to Victor 192

Chapter 24: The Love that Holds You Captive.............................. 198

Chapter 25: Anxiety's Ally.. 205

Chapter 26: Burning the Altar 213

Chapter 27: Spiritual Transformation 219

Chapter 28: Badge of Honor.. 226

Chapter 29: The Modest Woman... 230

Chapter 30: The Gatherer 235

Chapter 31: Discovering Your Inner Strength 248

Chapter 32: Embracing Our Beauty... 257

Chapter 33: Your Turn... 265

INTRODUCTION

Hi, I'm Robyn.
Accidental influencer
Serial entrepreneur
Safety guru
Podcast cohost
Public speaker
Mamma x4
Author

Essentially, I'm a little bit of everything. But hey, you will never get bored. I pride myself on being authentically me, even if that ruffles some feathers or means I occasionally overshare. From the pain and fear I experienced in my brutal sexual assault, leaving organized religion, and a devastating divorce, I have created purpose: I help other women navigate *their* pain and fear, teaching them how to turn those pains and fears into purpose.

My mission is to empower women—in their homes, starting businesses, becoming whole through healing, leaning into authenticity, or learning to fight back and kick ass. Looking for someone to be your "women kick butt" girl? Look no further.

Rising: *Fearless Women Rebelling*

To the women reading my book...

I am not different from you. The things that challenge you, hurt you, scare you, and keep you small are the same things that have kept me shackled to my own fears and beliefs.

If you are reading this book, that means I did it. I decided I was worthy enough to write. I was wise enough to teach. I was brave enough to lead. If you are reading this book, it means I escaped the chains of my own suffering.... and I DID THE DAMN THING. This means I can assist you in doing the same.

I need to lead with a disclaimer because I am going to be so frank. This book will not save you. This book has no secret answers. This book will not give you a quick way to "pass go". You may find this book hard to read. You may need to put it down for a moment. This book might piss you off.

But, I urge you to pick it back up. Then move forward, just as I have, just as we women do.

Disclaimer

If this is hard to read, then I wrote this book <u>FOR YOU</u>! Because like me, you have had enough.

In this book, I will open up my heart, soul, experience, history, and future to guide you on your journey. In exchange for my vulnerability and harsh honesty, I ask you to be open to recieving the message my book will hand to you because this message is from GOD.

I am not the author of this book. I am the vessel through which his words flow into this book. The things that impact your heart and soul from this book are not from Robyn Williams.
 They are from God.

The deepest message of this book is:

> *No one is coming to save you.*

> No man, no church, no outside source will save you.

> YOU have the power within to save yourself.

> It is *your* love for you that will save you.

> You have everything you need to save you.

> You are safe because of YOU.

> You are *saved* because of you.

> You are protected because of you.

> You are loved because of you.

TRIGGER WARNING

This book contains content that may be distressing or triggering for some readers. It discusses difficult topics, including abuse, divorce, and sexual assault. Reader discretion is advised. Please take care of your mental and emotional well-being as you read. If you feel overwhelmed at any point, consider pausing and seeking support from a trusted individual or professional.

To those who attempted to silence me with threats and legal intimidation, know this: your attempts to stifle my voice have only strengthened my resolve. This book, born from my truth and my journey, will be published despite your efforts to keep it buried. You may try to hide the light, but I will rise, and my story will shine through. My words are my power, and I will not be silenced. This is not just my victory; it is a triumph for every woman who dares to stand up, speak out, and rise above the fear of those who wish to keep her down.

Rising: Fearless Women Rebelling

PRELUDE

Where does someone just begin to write a book? Do I start at my traumatic divorce from my high school sweetheart? Maybe I could lead with my departure from the high-demand Mormon church and how my neighbors don't give me Christmas gifts anymore. My brutal sexual assault while running alone is always a good hook. . . . Plot twist: he is rotting in prison.

But what if it just started with . . .

Hi, I'm Robyn and I'm sick of the bullshit women have to deal with. I'm sick of the fear that governs our generations.

Whoops! I gave up my biggest secret: that I swear like a sailor while simultaneously serenading my babies to sleep with lullabies. An unhinged potty-mouth mother? Yep. And you will unapologetically either love me or hate me.

But spoiler alert: if it's the latter, it's because there is something in me that you have in you and you haven't found it yet because of fear. Maybe you want to be unapologetically honest? Maybe you want to write a book? Maybe you want to leave a marriage? Whatever it is, I'm going to challenge you to stick around because in MY book, I am not leaving chapters unpublished. I am not taking my mother's advice and leaving *parts* out of this book. I am speaking my truth, even if it makes you uncomfortable or embarasses my family. So get ready to read the thing that's about to single-handedly blow up my family's text thread. I don't leave chapters of my life unseen. I no longer omit parts of me. And you aren't going to leave out parts of *you* anymore, either.

If we are going to walk this path together, then we should get to know each other. I'll go first.

I'm Robyn.
Also known as Rob, Roberto, Rob-dawg, and Hoobaskank (don't ask).

I am a divorced mother of four small children, serial entrepreneur, and CEO/cofounder of several companies.

When I'm not burning casseroles or changing dirty diapers, I'm running several businesses and chasing my dreams as an entrepreneur. Outside of motherhood, my biggest passion is empowering and protecting women through safety advocacy, gathering like-minded women together to grow and heal, and having fun!

I feel like my healing journey has been a series of cycles. Once I feel like I have my trauma under control . . .

Bam! a brutal sexual assault (he is rotting in prison);
Bam! dealing with spouse's addictions, lies, and betrayal;
Bam! friendship loss;
Bam! family betrayal;

Introduction

Bam! faith expansion and transforming out of organized religion;
Bam! a devastating divorce;
Bam! single mothering;
Bam! dating again #terrifying;
Bam! finding love again . . . and I've never been happier.

The truth is, my healing journey never really started or ended. It's a constant state of going within, healing, being self-aware, forgiving, and experiencing grief, loss, and love.

I am a lot of things, and I pride myself on being them all authentically. My story is long and the plot twists are crazy. Grab a bag of chips, settle in, and hang on. It's nothing short of entertaining, messy, unexpected, and beautiful.

I know it's hard for you to believe life could get any better. I know the feeling when the last drop of hope slips through your hands, hits the floor, and dries up before your eyes. I know the eerie feeling that something is *wrong* in your relationship, yet you're constantly reassured "it's fine." I know well the decision to self-betray those thoughts and move forward, as if doing so is your only option. I have been there, and through *rising* through it all, I found a magical energy vortex of joy in life that I never knew existed. Without those doubts, lies, insecurities, and fears, I would never be able to experience joy—the kind you feel in hallmark life moments, like having a child or getting married.

I see joy everywhere now. It's hard for me to explain, but I feel so compelled to help you see this too. I'm pleading for you to experience this. It's almost as if it's this top secret feeling and I need to make sure everyone knows it exists. Before now, I was typically always "happy." But this transcends happiness and makes it look miniscule. Imagine that HIGH when you welcome a child into the world. That tangible JOY that feels as if God is truly allowing you into Heaven in those moments. It's as if for a moment of time everything stops and you are consumed with love, enthrallment, hope, peace, empathy, and pure bliss. It's the kind of experience you only have a handful of times in a lifetime. I feel those moments every day now, and I want you to RISE and experience them as well.

I no longer chase those "joyous" temporary highs that would occasionally hit like a drug—the kind I would search for like a strung out druggie who needed one more pill to make it through. One more "happy" memory to stay in my marriage. One more "hit of peace" to calm my soul, which knew "the embarking" was approaching. I won't settle for the mediocre "happy" I used to feel as a baseline. I have raised my standard and urge you to be open to the idea that there is more to feel at a deeper level. "Happy" doesn't have to be our standard anymore. There is *joy* that is WAITING for us to step into it. Joy sits in the simplest moments and it's HOPING you will be ready to see it. This level of daily exposure to God's miracles comes at a price, of course. You must be willing to walk through fire and then rise up to be able to recognize what a miracle it is to simply *be*. The *miracles* don't come and go; it's the *ability to recognize them* that is fleeting.

Recognition is the price.

CHAPTER 1

A GROVE, BUT MAKE IT PLEASANT

Growing up, life was pretty "normal." I was raised in a good home with good parents and semi-cool siblings. I can say that because I know they won't read this book, lol. Because family is the best group of supporters, right? Nah, that's bullshit and I'm going to be brave enough to say it (Don't kill me mama! I do love you, but you suck sometimes).

I grew up in a cozy community in Pleasant Grove, Utah and honestly, it was *pleasant*. We weren't rich, but we were only sometimes poor and I enjoyed MOST of my memories as a child. I was the fourth of five children and life was really normal, except for the few times my grandpa stuck his hand up my shirt and fondled me. Oh wait, I was supposed to leave that part out. I was supposed to forget about that and move along as if it never happened. The only problem with that is, the truth always RISES. No matter how far, deep, or wide you bury it, the truth will find a way up. And I could never title this book *Rising* if I wasn't willing to RISE **myself.**

I was a fun-loving kid who found adventure wherever I went. Happiness and joy were the co-parents that existed in our home. My mother was often singing and dancing in the kitchen or baking cookies to serve up nice and warm to us. We were a tight-knit family that got along for the most part and truly lived the American dream. We went to church, lived in a middle-class home, had enough money to play organized sports and go on one family vacation a year. From the outside, it truly seemed as if I had a picture-perfect childhood. But there was a side to my childhood that remains a forever reminder of the shackles that were placed upon me from the time I was a young age.

When I think back on my childhood, I think of the paddle my parents sometimes took to my rear end. When I was disobedient, lazy, wrong, or snappy, I was occasionally met with a swift spank or wooden spoon. But the spank or the spoon wasn't the authority in the home. FEAR WAS.

Fear was the dictator over how I chose to behave. Fear made my decisions:

> *Fear* I would disappoint my parents;
> *Fear* I would not make it to heaven;
> *Fear* I wouldn't be with my family forever;
> *Fear* I wouldn't be "worthy" enough for a man of God;
> *Fear* I would send my life on a dark trajectory if I didn't simply obey.

This wasn't necessarily my parents' fault. They were governed by this same backhanded fear. But I won't rob them of their accountability and say that their generational fear wasn't placed, tenfold, upon my head. They never took care of their fear, and unbeknownst to them, they gave it to me in a big shiny box.

Fear followed me into high school. It was my closest friend. I didn't kiss boys or drink alcohol. I never snuck out, missed curfew, or earned anything less than a 3.9 GPA. Fear kept me in line. Now that I think about it, fear did a fucking good job at raising me. As a teen, I was never a problem for my parents, but that came with consequences. I never saw a penis until my wedding day, when I was twenty years old. I mean, come on.

I guess you could say I was the perfect teen. But you know what they say: if the baby never cries, he will be a terrible toddler. If the teen doesn't send their parents to the looney bin, when that teen grows up and is in their thirties, they will write an unapologetic book that will disrupt the entire family heritage.

Damn. *Sorry mom.* It probably would have been better if I had just seen the penises back then.

Fear stayed with me my entire childhood. **It helped me play safe, which meant I would *stay* safe.** Fear made me loud, but not loud enough to be heard by anyone outside myself. Fear made me conform to what everyone else was doing. Fear kept me small, yet similar enough to fit right in. Honestly, I kinda started to really rely on fear. It had my back and I was committed to it. I hardly ever dated as a teen or young adult, but I didn't need to. I was in a committed relationship with fear. It was an unhealthy and toxic relationship, but it also worked disgustingly well. ... Kinda sounds like my first marriage. But wait, let's not jump ahead.

The first time I let someone down remains vivid in my memory. As a senior on the high school drill team, I held the esteemed position of secretary. Don't giggle—it was important. Who else would make the scrapbooks at the end of the year? My mornings were structured around waking up early, ensuring I never missed a beat—especially practice. However, on this one particular morning, I awoke with a start, realizing I had slept through my alarm and missed the entire first hour of drill team practice.

Panic surged through me as I imagined facing the wrath of our nineteen-year-old coach, who wielded authority that felt intimidating at the time. Instead of immediately owning up to my mistake and calling her to explain, I succumbed to the fear of disappointing her and my teammates. I knew if I was convincing enough, I would escape the consequences of running the track and forever sealing my doom as a loser.

Approaching Coach, I could palpably feel her initial anger. Without giving her a chance to speak, I dropped to my knees and launched into a meticulously crafted story.

> "Angela, I am so sorry I am late. I have never missed a practice nor been a millisecond late, but this morning on the way here a tree had fallen in the road and I was unable to drive around it. I had to wait until someone came to move it and my cell phone was dead, so I couldn't call you and—please give me mercy

because this was not my fault! And I'm never late, so obviously it would have to be something insane for me to be one hour late."

It worked.

She believed my story, and in that moment my fear of being seen as fallible saved me from immediate consequences. It wasn't fear that lied; it was me. Yet, paradoxically, by succumbing to fear, I escaped trouble and preserved my image.

This experience marked a pivotal moment when fear became an unwitting ally, shielding me from accountability.

It taught me the dangerous allure of avoiding vulnerability and the lengths to which fear can compel us to deceive ourselves and others. Despite this, I found a strange comfort in fear becoming my silent partner, shielding me from judgment and *preserving a façade of perfection.*

This book transcends my personal journey. It's a call for every woman to embrace the chapters they were told not to write. It's about breaking free from the shackles of generational trauma, passing on a torch of liberation through shared stories. Together, we dismantle the fear that holds us back from sharing our raw, unfiltered truths, forging a path to collective empowerment and healing.

CHAPTER 2

THE TRAIL OF DISCERNMENT

Growing up in the sheltered environment my mother meticulously crafted, safety was an omnipresent concern. Our home was fortified with locked doors and cautionary tales about potential dangers, instilling in me a heightened vigilance from an early age. While these measures were undoubtedly rooted in my mother's deep love and concern for our well-being, they inadvertently shaped my perception of the world through the lens of fear.

As a child, I internalized my mother's anxieties and became hyper focused on improbable threats like kidnapping or assault. What began as prudent caution gradually morphed into a pervasive fear that colored my everyday experiences. Despite the reassurances of statistical safety and the rare occurrence of such events, my mind fixated on the possibility, fueled by the constant reminders of vulnerability and danger.

Reflecting on my upbringing, I now recognize that my mother's teachings, while well-intentioned, were imparted through fear rather than empowerment. Her protective instincts, though understandable, inadvertently nurtured a mindset where fear overshadowed resilience and self-assurance. Instead of equipping me with tools to navigate the world confidently, I was conditioned to view it as a perilous landscape where danger lurked around every corner.

Ironically, this environment of heightened awareness did not shield me from tragedy. At eighteen, while innocently running alone, I became a victim of a brutal sexual assault—an experience that shattered the illusion of safety my mother had strived so hard to create. In the aftermath of this traumatic event, I couldn't help but see the cruel irony: the very danger my mother had sought to protect me from had manifested into a harsh reality.

This realization prompts a profound question: Are we the creators of our own fears? Did my mother's well-intentioned efforts to shield me inadvertently invite the very danger she feared most? It's a troubling thought, suggesting that our fears, when nurtured and internalized, can shape our realities in unexpected ways.

Yet, amid this introspection, I am also discovering a path to healing and understanding. Fear, I've come to realize, is a natural response to perceived threats, but it doesn't have to dictate our lives. We must strike a balance between caution and empowerment—acknowledging risks without allowing them to paralyze us.

In sharing my story, I hope to challenge the notion that fear must govern our existence. It's a call to embrace empowerment over fear, to cultivate resilience in the face of adversity, and to reclaim agency over our narratives. By confronting our fears with courage and compassion, we can transform them from creators of limitations into catalysts for growth and personal empowerment. This journey isn't just about overcoming trauma; it's about reclaiming a sense of security and forging a future where fear no longer defines who we are or what we can become.

During most people's lunch breaks, I was fighting for my life.

February 27, 2008, started as a normal day for me. I didn't realize that only four hours after my morning alarm went off, I would be fighting for my life on a public trail.

That morning was very similar to every other. I was a second-semester freshman attending college at Southern Utah University. Life was going well for me. I excelled in my science classes, hoped to become a dental hygienist, and I loved dancing on the university dance team.

As part of our training program on the dance team, we were expected to run a few miles a day to keep our cardio in check. This was something I enjoyed doing, and I had been going to the local gym during the winter season to get my miles in. This year in particular seemed to be a shorter winter, and on this bright February day, it felt as if spring had surprised us early. It was one of the first warm days of the season, and I wasn't the only one excited to be outside enjoying it.

The Trail of Discernment

I asked my roommate if she would go running with me after our morning classes. She agreed to do so, and then off to school we both went. When I got home around noon, she mentioned she had been called in to work and would no longer be able to go running with me.

No problem, I thought. I felt conflicted because I had never been running alone before. I knew it wasn't the safest thing to do, but I was now a grown woman not living with my parents. Wasn't it time I finally spread my wings to fly and stop being scared of everything?

When I was growing up, my mom was very safety-aware. I was convinced that, because of the safety awareness my mom had taught me, I was the most prepared and aware eighteen-year-old on campus. I battled myself for some time about whether I should skip the run or step into my power and realize I was fine to run alone. After all, I was living in what I thought was the safest city in Utah. It was likely there would be people outside, and I knew a safe place to run.

I ultimately decided it was best to get my miles done outside and that I would be fine. Though I didn't feel confident in running alone, I also felt I had been parented by fear, so this was me being brave.

I walked to a familiar place that my roommates and I enjoyed running. It was called the Canyon Trail. It was a popular, fairly new, paved leisure trail that ran through the city and gradually went about one mile up into the canyon. It was well-groomed and it was a place I felt safe. I was familiar with it and had run it many times before winter had hit. The trail wound through local baseball diamonds and parks. The last mile of the trail as you went into the canyon ran parallel to the highway. Once the trail started into the canyon, a river ran between the highway and the trail. I can't emphasize enough how widely popular and occupied this trail was. Even once you got into the final mile stretch of a more rural canyon landscape, you could almost always be seen from the highway at any given time.

It took me about twenty minutes to walk from my home to the trail, and I always used the excuse that walking instead of driving was my warm-up. As I walked to the trail, I remember being aware of the warm sun beating down on me and the many other people who were out enjoying the sunshine.

Once I was at the trail, I began to run. Clueing into my safety skills, I made sure to be aware of my surroundings. I noticed there were ten or so people on the trail with me. I remember seeing an older grandma walking her dog, another girl running alone, and some kids from the track team running in a cluster.

Within the first few minutes of running, I realized I had left my cell phone at home. This wasn't ideal for me because that is how I listened to music. Because it was a twenty-minute walk home, I decided to do the run musicless. As I ran, I kept having a strong feeling: *go home and get your cell phone*. I ignored it and picked up my pace. Again, I heard, *go home and get your cell phone*. No. I was going to quickly get this done. Again, *go home AND GET YOUR CELL PHONE*. I heard this deep-feeling voice another three to four times until it finally stopped me in my tracks. I needed to go home and get my cell phone, but I wasn't sure why.

I remember naïvely thinking that I was supposed to go get my phone in case the boy I liked had texted me. After all, if a boy texts you to make plans with him and you don't answer quickly, then he will ask the next available girl. This was why I thought I needed to have my phone—in the event I got asked out on a date. With this realization, I quickly turned around and headed home.

Once I was back home, I found my phone on my pillow. You will not believe what was waiting on my home screen: a text message from the hunk of a boy I had an obsession with! And he had asked me out! I remember being ecstatic to see this message and also so happy I had listened to myself and gone home to get my phone. *This* must be why I felt so strongly about returning home to get it. Plot twist: this hunk is now my fiancé, sixteen years later.

I remember responding to the text message, and he asked me what I was doing right then. I responded that I was going to the Canyon Trail to finish my run. He responded, "You shouldn't run alone." I told him I would be just fine and would be done in the next hour.

To be honest, I didn't want to go back to the trail and finish my run. I figured I had already exercised for about a half hour, so that would equate to the three miles we had to run. This logic didn't last long because I realized I couldn't lie to my coach when I had only run part of the requirement. So, with much less gumption than I'd had the first time, I headed back to the trail.

This time, I didn't feel the same as I originally had. As I was walking back to the trail, now at about 12:45 in the afternoon, I felt weird. I remember feeling anxiety specifically about an extremely random potential event. The last time I had been on this trail, a wild horse (or maybe it belonged to someone) had come barreling down the trail and almost trampled everyone in its path. I suddenly found myself having super intrusive thoughts about what I would do if another horse happened to come running down the trail.

As I filled with panic and fear, I was simultaneously completely convincing myself of how outrageous I sounded. A horse was not going to trample me, and I was going to be just fine. I finally reached the trail and began to run again. Though I felt uneasy, I didn't have a logical reason *why* I felt so strange. I noticed there were still plenty of people on the trail, and with all the courage I could muster, I began running.

It wasn't even five minutes in when, as I rounded a corner, I suddenly saw a large shadow approaching me. The horse! Startled and completely horrified, I jumped into the bushes off to the side of the trail to hide. As the "horse" came barreling around the corner, I realized it was *not* a horse but a large, muscular man riding a longboard.

When the man on the board saw me, he quickly stopped and jumped off to help the woman lying in the bushes.

"Are you okay?" he asked me as he held a hand out to help me stand up.

I was mortified. I had sagebrush in my hair, dirt on my hands, and had made the biggest fool of myself in front of a guy I then recognized as one of the star baseball players from the university. I remember feeling absolutely stupid and mortified that my paranoia and fear had caused such a scene.

We exchanged names. I learned his name was Casey.

"Are you sure you're okay?" Casey asked once more.

I assured him that lying in bushes was something I did frequently and that I was totally fine. He could tell my answer was absolutely bogus and reluctantly said goodbye and jumped back onto his board.

I was humiliated and so upset with myself. What was wrong with me? Why was I so startled and scared and jumping into bushes? As I stood there regaining my composure and brushing the dirt off myself, I noticed Casey had finished his ride and gotten into his car and left. I waited where I was until he was gone, so I wouldn't make a fool of myself again.

Robyn, pull yourself together. You are just fine. There are no horses. You are fine. Stop being such a scared girl. Nothing is going to happen, I reassured myself, and I took off to finish the last mile up the canyon.

Because I was familiar with the trail, I knew that the last few hundred feet of the trail started to incline and then stopped dead. The trail was going to end about a half mile up ahead, and I would just have to turn around. I knew I was in the final stretch, so I mustered up my courage and energy and hit the pavement running. I passed a person or two and didn't make much eye contact.

As I came around one of the final bends, I noticed a man walking down the trail. I immediately knew something was off with him, mainly because of how he was dressed. It was warm outside, and he was dressed in a beanie, large jacket, cargo pants, and hunting or military-style heavy boots, and he was carrying a backpack. I remember thinking, *He doesn't look like he is exercising.* Something felt off immediately, but he was quite a ways up ahead of me. I was headed up the trail and he was headed down.

We finally crossed paths. As we briefly passed one another on the trail, I turned to look at him. Immediately, my heart dropped. I knew something was off. They say you can see a man's soul through his eyes, and I knew something bad was about to happen.

I ripped out my earphones so I could hear what he was doing, and I quickly turned around to get a better look. I assumed I would only see his backside as he was walking down the trail, but I was shocked to see he had turned around and was headed back up the trail. Was he following me? Panic filled my body. He was following me. Or maybe I was just judgmental and he was just doing some sort of relay on the trail or forgot something.

Intuition is the ability to know something is wrong without needing any proof. It's something everyone has. You do not have to be baptized in a church to have this gift. It does not go away at midnight. It does not leave you, ever. My intuition was telling me something very bad was about to happen. But my logic was trying to convince me otherwise. I had conflicting thoughts that went between *this man is about to hurt me* and *maybe I am just crazy and judgmental.*

I turned back again to see where he was, and he was jogging behind me. He *was* following me. My palms began to sweat. My heart was racing, and my thoughts were all over the place.

Oh my gosh, this man is following me.

He is going to hurt me. I know it.

You are so judgmental, Robyn. He hasn't even said a word to you. He is out on a run, just like you.

No, he is chasing after me. I need to do something. What do I do?

It's the middle of the day. There are people on this trail. There is no way a random stranger would do anything to you right now. Look, there are cars on the highway. People can see you. You're fine.

No, I'm not. He turned around once he saw me. He is following me. He is after me.

Unsure of what I felt, I sprinted up the final stretch of the incline and reached the dead end.

I turned around to look at the man who was now standing on the trail, legs spread as if to block the trail, his hands in his pockets. He was laughing at me.

I was so confused and creeped out. I was unsure what I should do next. I looked to my right, and there was a twenty-foot drop-off into the river. To my left was a canyon landscape with trees, hills, and brush everywhere. I knew I shouldn't go that way in the event he really did try to hurt me. The best and only option I had was to run as fast as I could back down the trail and toward him. I was hoping I had just freaked myself out and I would run right past him. Yes, that's what I should do. Just run as fast as possible right past him, and everything will be fine.

As I was about to start running, I felt the strong impression to call 911 on my phone. I resisted this feeling because I grew up knowing to never call 911 unless you were "already dead." This wasn't really what I was taught, but I was definitely warned as a child to never call unless it was serious.

I wasn't sure if this was serious or not. This man hadn't said a word to me, hadn't touched me, and was still thirty feet away. What would I tell the cops? "I think I'm about to be attacked"?

I resisted the feeling but ultimately punched 911 into my phone, pressed *dial*, and began to run.

I ran as fast as I could toward him and then down the trail. For a split second, I thought I had passed him. Before relief even had time to set in, he grabbed me by the throat and slammed me to the pavement. I landed hard on my back, and before I could even comprehend what was happening, he was on top of me. The wind was knocked out of me, and my phone had flown out of my hands. I never checked to see if 911 had even successfully connected.

We learn about fight-or-flight, but less commonly known responses are freeze and fawn. I was completely frozen. I don't know how long I stayed like that, but terror and panic filled my entire being, rendering me incapable of making a sound or moving. I froze for ten seconds, forty seconds, maybe it was a minute. But what I did after coming out of the freeze helped save my life.

When I was twelve years old, I was excited to attend one of my first "Beehive" activities at my church. This was an exciting milestone as a teen. One of the activities they hosted on a Tuesday night was with a panel of about ten women who came to teach us important life skills.

They each only had five minutes to share their message.

One lady taught us how to change a diaper, which I have used thousands of times as a mother of four. The next lady taught us how to make a green smoothie. (I hope you can *hear* the sarcasm—I've never made that green smoothie.) Another lady spoke on how to sew a button onto a collared shirt, which I've also never done. The last lady had an interesting topic: self-defense and safety. She spoke for five minutes, and what she said went in one ear and out the other . . . or so I thought. I remember turning to my friend McKenzie and saying, "This will never happen to us."

Fast forward to that canyon trail, six years later. I was lying on my back, in the middle of the day, being brutally assaulted by a strange man I had never seen before. The lady's voice came into my head: "Yell your name and your location." The first thing I did after I unfroze was yell, "Robyn Williams! Canyon Trail! I'm being raped! Robyn Williams! Canyon Trail! I'm being raped!" over and over as loud as I could while still trying to stay alive. I didn't know if 911 had picked up the call, but I knew there were people on the trail not far below, and I was begging for someone to hear me and come help.

As I struggled to get away, I had a chance to grab my phone and see that 911 was connected. I screamed with all the breath in my lungs, "HELP ME! HELP ME! ROBYN WILLIAMS, CANYON TRAIL! I'M BEING RAPED!" The call ended. The man, realizing what I was doing, snatched the phone out of my hands and disconnected the call. My lifeline was now gone. The tiny amount of hope that had entered me when I'd seized the phone had now quickly exited my body. All I felt was pure terror and a morsel of faith that someone on the phone or the trail had heard me and was coming.

I struggled to get away, which is very different from fighting back. There were times I was able to stand up, and he would grab my ponytail and throw me face-first into the pavement. There were times I swung my arms at him to defend myself, only to be met with a slap or backhand across the face. I was getting thrown across the pavement, pushed to the ground, dragged by my hair, and pinned down. I never stopped trying to escape. We were in a full-blown brawl, and he was winning.

To give you context, he was not a small man. He was 6'2" and 230 pounds. At the time, in my freshman, petite, 18-year-old body, I was only 115 pounds. He was twice my size.

He picked me up and began to pull me off the paved trail and into the sagebrush, rocks, and mountain landscape. The lady's voice came into my head again: "Never leave the location you are attacked." I trusted this advice and did everything in my power to be put down. I kicked, arched, spat, head-butted, bit, and scratched. Ultimately, he only dragged me fifteen feet or so off the trail. I imagined I was a 600-lb trout and just flopped and flipped in his arms like a fish out of water would do. I fought like hell to stay right where I was. I knew that I had called for help, and if he took me somewhere else, no one would come for me.

He took off the backpack he had on and kept trying to get inside it. I had a strong impression that whatever he was so eagerly trying to get was bad, and I should do anything to stop him. I kicked the bag, pushed it, and threw it anytime he tried opening it one-handed. As he had one hand wrapped around my throat, strangling me, he was using the other to open the backpack. Off the trail and in the uncomfortable landscape of dirt, rocks, thorns, and bushes, he was successful in violently sexually assaulting me.

Though I continued to fight and try to escape, he was able to overpower me.

As he was lying on top of me, with one hand strangling me, he retrieved a large hunting knife from his bag. As he pressed it to my neck, I used one free hand to press against it as it quickly came closer to entering my throat.

Everything started to go fuzzy. I was losing consciousness because of the lack of oxygen, and I was running out of energy and courage to escape. I remember thinking to myself, *I hope my parents find my body. I hope my parents find my body*. I was certain at that moment that I was going to die.

Suddenly, my fear and pain transmuted into peace. I felt an immense softness, warmth, and peace that everything was going to be okay, and that I would see God soon. I felt okay to stop fighting and lean into this peaceful feeling. As I was fading into the comfort of the warmth, and likely the lack of oxygen, I had the clear thought to say a prayer. In my head, I said, "Heavenly Father, help me. I need help, and I don't know what to do."

Immediately, as if He was just waiting for me to ask, I heard, "Go for his groin." I paused and thought to myself, *but I've never touched a groin. I don't want to do that.* Again, I heard, "Go for the groin."

I wasn't sure how to do that. I was still using one hand to hold onto the knife and prevent the attacker from slitting my throat, and my other hand was pinned down underneath his body. I felt a shift in his weight and realized that, with enough force, I could potentially slide my hand out. I knew it was my only chance, so without knowing how or what to do, I went for it. I am not sure if I grabbed, twisted, pulled, or pinched, but it worked. He immediately let go of my throat and dropped the knife.

"Go for the eyes," I heard next. Instinctively and without much thought, I stuck my thumb into his eye and gouged at it as hard as possible. My force must have been stronger than I felt capable of, and when I realized the damage I had caused to his eye, I blurted out, "I'm sorry."

I'm sorry. *I* am sorry? I just told a man who had beaten the shit out of me, sexually assaulted me, and tried to kill me, "I'm sorry"? Did I actually just say "I'm sorry"? I just said "I'm sorry"! I'm FUCKING SORRY?!

What a showcase of my female programming to apologize in an event like this. I'm *not* sorry. I am absolutely *not fucking sorry*. And you will never be sorry, either, if you have to defend yourself or fight for your life. Promise me now. You will not apologize for defending yourself. You will not apologize for saying no. You will not apologize for fighting back. I am not fucking sorry. We are not fucking sorry.

He immediately released me and hit the ground, and I knew this was my last chance to get away. With the little strength I had left, I jumped to my feet to take off running. As I turned to run, he grabbed my left hand. I knew this was my last shot. If I got back on the ground, I was a dead girl. Without realizing what I was doing, I swung my body and right arm around as quickly as possible and aimed for his mouth. Two of my fingers struck the inside of his mouth like a fishhook to his cheek, causing damage to the corner of his mouth. He dropped to the ground again, and I spun around and ran as fast as I could.

Trauma is an interesting thing. In the most traumatic moment of my life, I remember clearly the thoughts I was having as I was running from a man who had tried to take my life. I was beaten, bloody, and not fully clothed.

I was a dancer at the university, and most of my friends were on the track team. They always teased me because I was a slow runner and could never keep up with their college records. They called me "Rudy." As I was running for my life down a public trail, still in the middle of the day, I remember green trees flashing by. I realized I was running at what I would consider a superhuman speed. I was going so fast that I could not see the details of the trees, only a green blur as I ran down the trail.

Like a mother who can lift a car off a child in an emergency, my adrenaline was racing. I had to have run a five-minute mile. Despite fighting to stay alive just moments before, I was boasting in my head that *if my friends could see me now, I would be recruited onto the track team, no doubt.* I still find it so bizarre that this was the thought I was having as I ran for my life. Trauma, man. It's fascinating.

Trauma doesn't end with escape. It must be processed physically, mentally, emotionally, and psychologically. And boy, was there a lot to process.

CHAPTER 3

GOODBYE TO MY FORMER SELF

As I ran down the trail at lighting speed, I came around the corner and was startled to see a man standing in my way. He was a strong, fit, twenty-something-year-old with tattooed arms. He was shouting my name and flagging me down to stop running. When I realized who it was, my first thought was judgmental. *He is here to hurt me. Why is he back on the trail? I saw him get in his car and drive away.*

"ROBYN, ROBYN, STOP. IT'S OKAY. IT'S ME, CASEY."

The longboarder, who I had mistaken for a horse earlier, was back on the trail and trying to get me to stop and talk with him.

I was convinced Casey was there to hurt me and that he was in cahoots with the man I just fought my life for. Why else would Casey be back?

"If you are here to help me, throw me your cell phone," I cried out to him as I backed away from him.

He slowly slid his phone across the pavement to me, scooted off the trail so I could pass, and allowed me to run past him.

I didn't realize until later how much of a miracle it was that Casey had come back to the trail.

While in another full sprint, I dialed 911 into Casey's phone, desperate for someone to pick up.

They did, and they had heard everything up until my attacker had hung up. They were only minutes away and had sent their entire fleet of police officers, fire trucks, and ambulances to come find me.

They told me to meet them at the bridge. I had already passed that and was not going to turn around and run back toward where my attacker likely still was, so I climbed down the ravine, trudged through the river bank, and climbed onto the highway.

I still remember it like it was from a movie scene. As I ran up to an approaching cop car, he stopped quickly, got out, and opened his arms. Just as if he were my father, I collapsed into his embrace. I remember him saying "You're safe now. You're safe. Everything is okay. I have you. You're safe."

I was unable to speak because of the hysteria and panic that had flooded my body, and though he needed to question me to find out where the attacker was, he held me for just long enough that I could catch my breath.

Within moments, the ambulance pulled up and I was whisked away into a red rectangle with flashing lights, and we bolted into town. People surrounded me in the ambulance assessing my injuries, putting oxygen on me, and poking and prodding me, but I remember one woman's face. She continued to calmly reassure me that everything would be fine.

I realized I had wet and soiled my pants sometime during the assault and, feeling embarrassed, I told her, "I am so sorry. I think I wet my pants. And maybe something else."

She grabbed my hand and said, "Don't worry, sweetie. I would have done the same thing. You are so brave. Everything is going to be okay."

Before I knew it, I was in a cold sterile hospital room filled with police officers. Everything was so overwhelming and all I wanted was my family. The police asked for my dad's phone number, but I could not remember it. My attacker still had my phone and I had hit my head on the pavement so many times I was unable to recall all of my dad's number.

Cops and nurses were coming in and out and I was running on high adrenaline. Realizing I was safe now, I was unable to comprehend the severity of what had just happened. I remember cheerfully telling each nurse and officer, "I am okay. It doesn't hurt. I'm fine. Can I go home now?" I realized it was now later in the afternoon and I was supposed to be teaching a hip hop class to sixth graders. I kept saying, "I have work. I need to leave. Can you please discharge me so I can get to work?"

The nurse quietly giggled and assured me I would not be going to work or home anytime soon. They had me undress and they collected any items I still had on or with me to take into evidence. As I sat there naked under a thin hospital gown, I remember feeling upset that they took my favorite pair of running shoes away. I still wish I had been given back those shoes.

I remember being so confused about what had just happened. Was this truly real life? It was one of those out-of-body experiences as I sat there naked on the hospital bed and thought, *wait, did that really just happen*?

As I sat there alone and afraid, with my family hours away, the police detective questioned me, asking me to recount, in detail, what had happened, what my attacker looked like, and anything else I could recall. I wasn't sure my attacker had even been apprehended or if he had gotten away. Though I was alone and afraid, the two officers in the room with me were gentle, kind, and patient with my slow responses. Still to this day, I am very close with these officers. They were walking angels that day as I sat there in the most vulnerable and sacred moments of my life.

My adrenaline had numbed any pain and besides the obvious road rash, cuts, and blood, I wasn't sure if I was hurt. So the hospital staff took me to get X-rays to see if I had broken any bones.

When they wheeled me into the X-ray room, I was surprised to see that the X-ray tech was my roommate. We locked eyes with one another, and within moments, we both began to sob. It was the biggest tender mercy to have a familiar face there with me. She embraced me and told the accompanying officers she knew me and could help locate my family, roommates, and work.

After the X-rays, when I re-entered my hospital room, there was a new face sitting in the corner. She was a girl with brown hair who looked about a year or two older than me. They introduced her as a victim's advocate. She kindly introduced herself and told me she had a peach Adidas jumpsuit waiting for me to wear when I was done with my SANE kit (SANE stands for Sexual Assault Nurse Examination).

The encounter with the SANE nurse was a pivotal moment in the aftermath of my brutal assault—an experience that remains vivid in my memory for its blend of care and discomfort. As the SANE nurse introduced herself, her gentle demeanor and professional assurance provided a fleeting sense of safety amid the chaos. A registered nurse specially trained in handling sexual assault cases, she carefully explained each step of the examination process, from assessing injuries to documenting them in meticulous detail.

Starting at the top of my head, she methodically combed through my hair, collecting evidence and inspecting my head for any signs of trauma. Moving down my body with painstaking thoroughness, she examined every injury, cleaning and bandaging each one before carefully documenting it on paper. Her attention to detail was unwavering. She paused at my hands to meticulously scrape underneath each fingernail, preserving potential evidence in vials.

The process was clinical, necessary, yet profoundly invasive. She took many pictures and several swabs of my blood and other items from my body.

Although I was grateful for her taking such care and caution to document everything, I hated the part where she had to assess and swab my vagina and surrounding areas. I found myself enduring the uncomfortable reality of having my most intimate areas scrutinized and swabbed—a necessary but excruciatingly intimate ordeal that left me feeling exposed and vulnerable. In those moments, alone and without the familiar comfort of loved ones, I closed my eyes tightly, willing the examination to be over, grappling with the intrusion upon my already violated body.

Despite my discomfort, I deeply appreciated the nurse's expertise and dedication to documenting every detail. Her calm demeanor and respectful approach provided a semblance of dignity during a time when I felt anything but dignified. However, it's crucial to acknowledge that for many survivors, including myself, such examinations can be deeply unsettling, amplifying feelings of vulnerability and trauma in the immediate aftermath of an assault.

While I am grateful for the professionalism and care shown by SANE nurses, it's important to shed light on the discomfort and emotional toll these exams can impose on survivors. The intrusion upon one's body, already violated by violence, underscores the need for sensitivity and compassion in every step of the forensic process. These examinations are vital for justice and healing, yet they should be conducted with utmost respect for the survivor's emotional and physical well-being.

My experience reinforces the importance of advocacy for survivors, ensuring that they receive not only medical care but also compassionate support throughout the forensic examination process.

I have reconnected with the SANE nurse who worked on me and I can't emphasize enough how professional and also warm and trustworthy she was. I am very grateful for her work and how she treated me. She had a warm and friendly face during one of the most uncomfortable hours of my life.

After my exam, they let me put on the peach Adidas jumpsuit the advocate brought for me. It seemed to have been worn before. Maybe it was a donation? I was grateful to have it. The victim's advocate talked to me for a bit as I sat there waiting for my family to arrive. They were four hours away. Once my dad had made contact with the police, he and my mom jumped in the car and sped all the way down to southern Utah. My dad said he had never driven so fast in his life.

Once I was discharged from the hospital, the ordeal of my assault continued with a formal interview at the police station. I entered a small room and was greeted by a detective who, with solemn professionalism, guided me through the painful task of recounting the harrowing details once more. Each word felt like reliving the trauma, but I understood the gravity of providing a thorough account for justice to prevail. Despite the emotional toll, I summoned every memory, every detail, knowing it was all crucial to the investigation.

After the interview concluded, reality starkly set in. There was no return to normalcy, no chance to gather my belongings or bid farewell to the life I had known just hours earlier. My parents whisked me away, four hours back to their home, leaving behind everything—my clothes, personal items, and the people who had been part of my daily life. It was a sudden, unceremonious departure, devoid of closure or preparation.

The abruptness of leaving my college home meant I never got to explain to my roommates why I was disappearing, or inform my professors why I would no longer be attending classes. I couldn't face my university dance coach to explain my absence or reassure my students at the dance studio where I taught. In an instant, my freshman year, once filled with hopes and new beginnings, came to an abrupt halt.

Life as I knew it had irrevocably changed. The future I had envisioned, filled with dreams and aspirations, was now suspended in uncertainty. The familiar contours of my existence were replaced by a surreal landscape where every plan, every goal, and every expectation hung in limbo. The sudden rupture left me disoriented and grappling with the profound loss of the life I had taken for granted just a day earlier.

In that single day, the trajectory of my life shifted beyond recognition. What lie ahead was a journey through uncharted territory, navigating the aftermath of trauma while grappling with the shattered remnants of my former self. The abrupt departure symbolized not just physical relocation but an emotional and psychological upheaval that would shape my path forward, challenging me to rebuild from the ruins of shattered innocence and shattered dreams. And rebuild I did, digging a ditch of consequences for my attacker and building bridges of safety for millions of other women along the way.

CHAPTER 4

ONE LIFE SAVED, NOW MILLIONS

So, to the burning questions you're just wishing to ask . . .
Did they catch the man who did this?
What was Casey's involvement and why did he come back?

Casey came back to the trail simply because he was prompted to. He had finished longboarding the trail and was headed into town to have lunch with his fiancée. He felt the need to go back up to the trail once more, and though all logic defied reason for him to go back, he listened to the nudge and headed back up the trail.

While I was running for my life and met up with Casey, my attacker was still chasing after me. I didn't know this because I never turned back to look. After Casey threw his phone so I could call 911 and I kept running, Casey saw my attacker (with his knife still in his hand) and ran after him. What a brave man. My attacker, knowing he was about to be apprehended, started running into the hills to hide. Because Casey was there when the police arrived a short time later, he was able to direct the police to where the man was hiding. With snipers in the hills and officers pursuing with guns drawn, my attacker finally surrendered and came down from the hills.

He was taken into custody with my belongings—including my phone—and his knife still in his hands. It turns out, he had recently been released from prison for prior violent sexual crimes and had not reported to his parole officer. He was a wanted man with a long history of trouble and crimes.

He gave a full and detailed confession about what he did, why he did it, and what he was going to do had I not gotten away. It was bone chilling and detailed. The police chief at the time later told me, "I have never met someone so evil. Staring into his eyes, I knew he was pure evil and meant the things he said. Robyn, although I am sorry you had to endure this, I'm certain if it was any other woman that day, there would have been a dead girl on the trail. You fought like hell and we are so proud of you."

After many court hearings, countless meetings, and an anxiety-filled year for me as I waited for his mental competence to be determined, he ultimately pleaded guilty and was sentenced to fifteen years-to-life in federal prison. During the year I wrote this book, he reached the fifteen-year mark of his sentence.

The first few years were significant milestones, each year putting more distance between the attack and my ongoing journey of healing. Years one, two, and three marked early but crucial steps away from the trauma. By year five, I had made incredible strides in my recovery, feeling stronger and more empowered. Year ten was victorious for me;

I had dedicated a decade to helping thousands of women stay *prepared, not scared*—my tagline I use to instill confidence in women.

However, the fifteen-year mark filled me with fear. Would he be released? Could the system that had let him out once before make the same mistake again? The possibility loomed over me, casting a shadow on my hard-won peace.

Every five years I receive notifications from the state board of pardons and parole about the status of his incarceration. When he is eligible to speak at a parole hearing, I have the opportunity to send letters or a representative, or even attend in person to voice my reasons for why he should remain imprisoned. At the five- and ten-year marks, I sent letters. But year fifteen brought an overwhelming sense of dread. Would he get out this time?

The fifteen-year anniversary of his incarceration brought me a resurgence of anxiety and worry about his potential release. The uncertainty was suffocating. However, I was notified that due to his continued bad behavior, he would not be eligible for another hearing for a definite six more years. This news brought a temporary sense of relief, but it also highlighted the ongoing battle. Given that this was not his first offense, I have a strong hope that he will remain in prison for the rest of his life. I am confident he would reoffend if released.

This journey has taught me that healing is not a linear process. Each milestone, while significant, brings its own set of challenges and fears. The thought of his potential release is a constant reminder of the fragility of safety. Yet, it also strengthens my resolve to continue my advocacy work, ensuring that other women can find their own paths to empowerment and safety.

The fear that resurfaces with each parole hearing is a stark reminder of the lasting impact of trauma. Despite the progress I've made, the threat of his release underscores the importance of vigilance and advocacy. It is a testament to the resilience required to move forward while knowing that the past can resurface at any moment.

As I look forward to the next six years, I am committed to using my voice and my platform to ensure that he remains where he belongs. My fight is not just for myself but for every woman who has faced similar fears. It is a fight for justice, for safety, and for the right to live without the shadow of past trauma.

In this ongoing journey, I have learned that strength comes not just from overcoming the past but from continually standing up for what is right. The fear and anxiety are part of the process but so is the unwavering determination to protect myself and others. This experience has solidified my belief that, even in the face of uncertainty, we have the power to shape our own futures and to advocate for a world where justice prevails.

I am often asked, "If you could go back in time, knowing what was about to happen, would you still choose to run alone that day?" My answer, without hesitation, is yes. I would still go running alone. I would still fight for my life. I would endure it all again because that experience, as horrifying as it was, not only transformed my life but has also saved tens of thousands of women's lives.

It has shaped me into the woman I am today.

It has given my life a specific purpose and passion that I might never have discovered otherwise.

The strength and resilience I found within myself during and after that traumatic event have fueled my mission to empower and protect women everywhere.

This purpose has become a driving force in my life. It has led me to create programs, write books, and speak out about safety and self-defense. The impact of my work has been profound, touching the lives of countless women who have found strength, courage, and practical skills through my advocacy.

Knowing that my experience has equipped others to avoid similar dangers, to stand up for themselves, and to survive their own challenges is a source of immense fulfillment.

Every story of a woman who protected herself using the tools and knowledge I provided reaffirms that my suffering was not in vain.

It has all been part of a larger transformative journey that extends far beyond my own personal healing.

In hindsight, while the pain and fear were real and overwhelming, the outcome has been a testament to the power of turning trauma into triumph. This journey has taught me that even the darkest moments can be the catalyst for profound and positive change.

Would I willingly choose to face such an ordeal again? The answer is complex, wrapped in the undeniable truth that through adversity, we find our greatest strengths. I recognize that my path, as difficult as it has been, has illuminated the way for others. It has given me a voice and a platform to make a meaningful difference.

So, yes, I would still choose to run alone that day, not because I am unaffected by the trauma but because I understand the profound impact my survival has had on the lives of so many others.

This experience has imbued my life with a sense of mission and responsibility that I carry with me every day. It has forged a deep, unshakeable conviction that through our trials we can find purpose and create ripples of change that extend far beyond ourselves. My story is a testament to the fact that we have the power to transform our pain into a force for good, inspiring and protecting others along the way.

After fighting for my life that day, I decided to dedicate my purpose to protecting and empowering women, while he rots in jail. In that moment on the trail, the entire trajectory of my life's mission changed. I never wanted this to happen to my sisters, friends, and nieces. So, I began to train, learn, educate, and spread awareness. And I eventually created my own self-defense and awareness program called S.A.F.E. I never knew my mission and message would reach millions of women.

S.A.F.E. is an acronym that stands for
　S: Self-defense
　A: Awareness
　F: Fight Back
　E: Empowerment

One Life Saved, Now Millions

I taught my course in person for close to ten years. After years of traveling across the country to share my message and teach, I found myself increasingly frustrated by the limitations of being just one person trying to reach millions. How could I possibly connect with and empower every woman who needed my message?

The answer came in the form of my online S.A.F.E. course.

With a three-month-old newborn plus three older toddlers, and a crumbling marriage, I decided to teach myself how to create an online course. I had no idea where to begin. In the deep hours of the night, while breastfeeding my newborn, I drew upon my decade of advocacy for women and children, organizing my knowledge into a comprehensive library.

After six months of sleepless nights, I was finally ready to record my course. In my office, carrying twenty-five extra pounds of baby weight, with bags under my eyes and a less-than-perfect haircut, I recorded each module. Most of the time, my newborn was breastfeeding just inches away from the bottom of the camera shot. There was no camera crew, no makeup artist to cover my lack of sleep, and no teleprompter. It was just me and my own experience.

The prospect of marketing this course felt daunting. Despite my insecurities, I pushed forward. Although the course lacked professional polish, the knowledge it contained was invaluable. I began sharing it on social media, and people started enrolling. That original course, created in the humble setting of my office with the realities of motherhood on full display, generated over $100,000 in just two years. At the time, this felt quite substantial and was a major achievement for a self-produced, stay-at-home mom with saggy boobs and four children under the age of eight.

This experience taught me several profound lessons.

Timing is never perfect.
There is never a perfect time to start something life-changing. Even amid chaos and uncertainty, taking the first step is crucial. If you wait for ideal conditions, you may never begin.

Self-belief is key.
Even when you don't know where to begin or what to do, believing in yourself is essential. Confidence in your abilities and purpose can drive you to overcome any obstacle.

Purpose fuels persistence.
When you have a clear purpose, you can find a way to overcome challenges. My dedication to empowering women kept me going through sleepless nights and daunting tasks.

Authenticity matters.
While professionalism has its place, the authenticity of my initial recordings resonated with many. Sharing my real-life struggles and experiences made the content relatable and impactful.

Impact over perfection

The course's impact on thousands of women mattered more than its initial lack of polish. Hundreds of women have shared how the course saved their lives, proving that substance outweighs superficial perfection.

Since then, I've hired a professional camera crew, makeup artists, and teleprompter experts to re-record my course. It is now as polished and professional as possible while retaining the simplicity and authenticity of my experience in the safety and self-defense world.

S.A.F.E. is a go-at-your-own-pace digital course. With over 25 videos, you will be educated on ALL things safety, like

- running or hiking alone
- dating safety
- internet safety
- children's safety
- car safety
- traveling safety
- rideshare safety
- educating children
- combating anxiety
- and so much more!

Because you are reading my book, I want to give you access to my course for the same price as you and your bestie's starbucks order. Normally priced at $222, please enjoy my lifesaving course for $22. YES, TWENTY-TWO DOLLARS with code RISE22. Because this is such an incredible discount, I trust you will not share this code publicly or on social media or forums. Please, as my gift for reading my book, I hope you choose to join the course for $200 off, and keep this discount offer to yourself only.

And because every woman needs to know how to empower and protect themselves, please feel free to tell people ABOUT the S.A.F.E. course. Encourage every woman you know to either purchase the S.A.F.E course at the regular price of $222 (a low price for a high-value course), or purchase my book to learn how to empower themselves with the lessons they'll learn from reading and also gain access to the discount code for S.A.F.E.

Scan this QR code to learn more about my course and snag your deal.

Creating, recording, and believing in myself to produce this course is one of the proudest accomplishments of my life. Thousands of women have taken my course. Millions more will take it. Hundreds of those women who have taken the course have come back to tell me my course saved their lives. I know the information and messages in this course personally saved my life and will continue to save millions of lives.

In the end, this journey from my brutal sexual assault to traveling the world to empower women reinforced my belief that even the most challenging circumstances can be transformed into opportunities for growth and empowerment. By trusting in my purpose and persevering through the initial pain of my assault, in addition to the obstacles of being a mother while trying to reach others, I created something that has made a tangible difference in the world.

This experience taught me that our greatest sources of pain can become powerful catalysts for change. When I reflect on my journey, I am struck by how far I have come from those dark moments. My assault left me feeling shattered and powerless, but it also ignited a fire within me to fight for myself and others. The trauma could have defined and confined me, but instead it became the foundation upon which I built a mission of empowerment and education.

The process of creating my S.A.F.E. course was a testament to resilience and determination. Each sleepless night spent categorizing my knowledge, every moment of doubt and insecurity, was a step toward reclaiming my power.

The course is not just a compilation of information; it is a manifestation of my will to turn my pain into purpose.

As a mother, I faced unique challenges that tested my resolve. Balancing the demands of caring for my children, particularly a newborn, with the ambition to reach and help others was no small feat. Yet, in those quiet moments breastfeeding my child while brainstorming course modules, I found a profound sense of purpose. I realized that my experiences as a mother only enriched my message, grounding it in the reality of everyday struggles and triumphs.

The overwhelming response to my course has been both humbling and affirming. Knowing that thousands of women have found strength and safety through my teachings is a source of immense pride.

Each testimonial from a woman who felt seen, heard, and empowered reminds me why I embarked on this journey. It reminds me that if ever given a choice, I would still allow February 27th, 2008 to pan out the way it did. The knowledge that my course has saved lives is a testament to the power of turning personal pain into collective strength.

Looking ahead, I am committed to continuing this work, knowing that millions more women can benefit from the knowledge and support I offer. My journey has taught me that even in the face of adversity, we have the power to create change. By embracing our vulnerabilities and trusting in our purpose, we can transform our lives and the lives of others.

In the end, my journey from victim to advocate, from a mother struggling to find balance to a creator of a lifesaving course, exemplifies the transformative power of resilience. It is a reminder that no matter how insurmountable our challenges may seem, there is always potential for growth and empowerment.

By believing in ourselves and our purpose, we can turn our darkest moments into beacons of hope and change for the world.

CHAPTER 5

FEAR ISN'T THE LIAR . . . YOU ARE

It struck me as if my life was following a perfect script, having my worst nightmare come true.

Being parented by fear.

Getting in a relationship filled with constant fear.

A demanding religion where I excelled but lived in fear.

Fear of leaving . . . fear, fear, fear. *Was my generational trauma fear?*

In this book, I want you to challenge fear. I want you to ask it to step inside the ring and face you.

I am writing all the chapters of my book, setting the standard, and facing hate, potential legal battles, and challenges, yet standing strong in my truth. I want YOU to open your books to reveal the chapters you've been compelled to omit. Imagine a book's end with blank pages, urging women to write the chapters they've kept hidden, to share the untold stories. Well, since you're here and brave enough to read this book, that means you're ready to write the chapters you haven't shared with anyone. In the back of this book, I have left blank pages for you to write your untold chapters in and once you have, I want you to pass this book along to encourage other women to share their suppressed chapters. We will create a ripple effect until every woman's voice is heard. Together, we will collectively witness bravery.

Embarking on this journey is about confronting fear head-on, acknowledging it, and taking full accountability. Yes, there might be legal consequences, maybe even lawsuits, but how many women keep silent? I'm willing to take on that burden, be sued for every book sold, if it means millions of women can finally speak up. The more women who stand in their truth, the faster we will shut down the opposition. This is where the rebellion starts.

This is us starting the REBELLION OF FEARLESS WOMEN.

Ahh, sorry. I forgot to mention you were joining a rebellion. But, if you couldn't tell by the cover of my book—which makes it look like I'm pantless—and the very title of this book—which literally has the word "rebelling" in it—then honestly, if you're surprised, that's your bad.

Owning our fear is the first step to accepting it. We must allow it to coexist with us, rather than fighting it outright. You know when I told you to get into the ring with fear? Yeah, plot twist: I was never going to ask you to *fight* fear. Instead, I want you to sit down and greet fear, and start talking with it about the latest gossip. Actually no, no gossip. That shit ends here.

Anyway, instead of rejecting it, we women let fear sleep beside us because it creates an illusion of safety. What If I told you to make love with fear? If you're going to let it lie next to you, you may as well fu** it! Otherwise, why are you letting it into your bed? Use your fear for fuel. And in this case, let it be orgasmic freedom. This is what breaks you free from toxic patterns: not running from fear but fully being with it.

Acknowledging fear is how we find worth beyond these cycles.

Fear is not a liar. In fact, it's like the best friend who tells us we look fat in a dress. Fear tells the truth about our insecurities and anxieties. Fear is here to teach you something. If we truly want to break free from fear, we have to share what our fears *are*. Breaking free involves sharing these fears openly despite the discomfort. Living in fear is living a lie. The key to a breakthrough is to speak the truth *even when you're scared.*

Fear isn't the liar. The real lie is pretending fear isn't there.

Fear isn't a liar. You are.

Every woman has unique fears: not being loved, accepted, or enough; or maybe fear of walking in a dark parking lot alone; or fear of following your dreams. Maybe you have fear that you won't be able to have children. Maybe you have a fear that if you step away from religion, you will lose God. Maybe you have fear that if you leave your marriage, you will never survive. Maybe you have fear that you will shit your pants after you have Taco Bell.

Rising: Fearless Women Rebelling

Whatever your fears are, I am challenging you to SEE them. Stop running from them and write them down, right here, right now. After all, fear is already sleeping next to you.

Remember, you have the power to be fearless.

I am afraid of:

_____
_____
_____
_____
_____
_____
_____
_____
_____
_____
_____
_____
_____
_____
_____
_____
_____
_____
_____
_____
_____
_____

Owning the fears you just wrote about and being unapologetically authentic is liberating. Fear no longer controls me; the liberation of being unafraid and speaking the truth is what freed me, and it will free you.

Freedom is worth any price.

This book isn't just my story; it's an invitation for every woman to share the chapters they've been told not to write. The collaborative journey breaks generational trauma as you pass the book along like a torch. Together, we'll liberate ourselves from the fear of sharing the raw, unfiltered truth.

Even the desire for justice and liberation is often stifled by fear. Fear is the authority that silences us and keeps us from sharing what we should. This book is a commitment to 100% truth, and I challenge you to face the uncomfortable chapters within. This is a call to stop accepting incomplete versions of yourself and embrace the bravery of being the one who speaks up. The fear no longer rules me because I have chosen to speak my truth.

It's time you write the chapters that have been suppressed within you for too long.

Breaking free from these patterns, I realized I had been playing the characters of a story I no longer wanted to read. Now, as I declare, "Fear, you're out!"

>I take control.
>I write my book.

I make choices without being governed by anyone else's fear.

I am radically accountable for my actions.

I have been exonerated from my own shackles of fear and now stand as a liberated being.

Overcoming fear has been a recurring theme in my life, shaping who I am today. There have been two particularly liberating moments: overcoming my decade-long fear of flying and leaving my thirteen-year marriage. These experiences underscore the transformative power of confronting our deepest fears.

As a child, flying was a common and carefree activity for me. It wasn't until I was twenty-one that I developed a paralyzing fear of airplanes. I vividly remember the flight that changed everything. We were returning from celebrating my then-spouse's grandmother's 100th birthday. As we flew from Nevada to Utah, a massive storm hit the airport. All flights heading to Utah were grounded, except ours.

What began as a routine flight quickly turned into a nightmare. The turbulence was unlike anything I had ever experienced. It wasn't the mild shaking that lulls some passengers to sleep; it was a violent, heart-stopping ordeal that had everyone on board screaming and crying. The plane would drop suddenly, leaving us weightless before slamming back up again. The passenger next to me, who happened to be a pilot, looked as terrified as I felt.

Fear Isn't the Liar . . . You Are

I looked at my spouse, and in that moment, we exchanged what felt like our final goodbyes, assuring each other of our love. The fear was palpable.

As we approached the Salt Lake City International Airport, the plane's descent seemed to signal our salvation. Passengers began to cheer, relieved that we had made it. But just as we were about to touch down, the plane jerked violently upward, climbing back into the turbulent skies, as if a toddler had grabbed the cockpit joystick and pulled it quickly the opposite way.

We had not landed, and in fact were now going almost vertical back into the same air space that had just had us all questioning our gravestone dates. Several people started hysterically bawling and the collective thought was that either we had been hijacked or had missed the runway. They made no calls on the intercom, and for another thirty minutes as everyone waited in fear to find out where we were headed, absolute fear entered into me. Long story short, I didn't die in an airplane. But, after a traumatic emergency landing at the Denver airport, three hours stuck on the plane with people throwing up all over, bathrooms closed, anxious people yelling to get off, and one last flight back into Salt Lake . . . I vowed to never fly again. You know it was a really bad deal when the airline gave every passenger a thousand dollars in vouchers for future flights. Umm, no thanks. I'd rather drive to Hawaii.

For the next twelve years I adhered to that vow, driving everywhere to avoid airplanes. When flying was unavoidable, I was a mess of panic attacks and embarrassing outbursts. Turbulence, no matter how minor, would send me into a spiral of fear. I once ended up crying on a stranger's lap as she tried to comfort me. This fear owned me, dictating my actions and limiting my freedom.

It was overly embarrassing and a lot of work for those traveling with me. I had to be coddled, soothed, or straight-up told to shut up while I was PANICKING on the plane. I felt it was a fear I would never get over, and it was one that kept me tethered. I wanted to travel the world, but as we all know, I never drove to Hawaii.

When I tell you that accepting your fears is how you face them, I mean it. Now, I travel on airplanes twelve to twenty times a year. I fly so frequently that I now have access to sky clubs, and my main credit card I use is affiliated with an airline. But how? How did I get over this fear that had tethered me to the ground and caused a lot of anxiety and pain in me? I accepted the fear.

I accepted what it would feel like IF I died in an airplane.

During the grueling process of divorce, I was on a flight to Florida with my daughter. We had to go for her dance competition, and as much as I had tried to find a way to drive across the country instead, logistically we needed to fly. I was in emotional shambles from my marital split, and my zest for life was starting to dim. I was in a really dark place. In true Robyn fashion, as the first (and maybe only) bump in the air hit, anxiety and panic rushed into my body. I felt my body temperature rise. I started to cry and sweat. I let the fear into me, and I allowed it to start the toxic spiral I had become so familiar with. But this time, I had a thought come into my head.

If the plane crashed, it wouldn't be the worst way to die. I would go quickly. I wouldn't feel anything. I wouldn't have to deal with this divorce. My kids wouldn't be from a divorced family; they would just have a dead mom.

It was a morbid and unsettling thought, but it forced me to confront my fear head-on. I allowed myself to sit with the fear of dying in a plane crash. I accepted what it would actually look and feel like if this fear came true. I let it be with me. I planned my funeral in great detail. I imagined my children's lives without their mother. I visualized it, accepted it, and in doing so, found an unexpected peace. For the rest of the flight, I was calm. By accepting my fear, I had robbed it of its power over me.

Accepting my fear is how I got over it. Sitting with my fear and being with it is how I now fly all over the world.

When we sit with our fears and don't run from them, we call back all of our power.

This experience taught me a profound lesson:

The liberation from our fears is to truly see them, accept them, and sit with them.

By confronting my fear of flying, I reclaimed my power and opened up new possibilities for my life. Now, I travel frequently, flying around the world with a newfound sense of freedom.

The same principle applies to other fears. Writing this book has stirred up fears of its own—fear of repercussions from the Mormon church, my family, friends, and former partners. But just as I overcame my fear of flying, I must confront these fears too. My story deserves to be told honestly and unfiltered.

Fear is no longer my enemy; it is my guide. By embracing my fears, I stand my ground and claim my authority. This is the anthem of my soul, the declaration of my truth. As I write these words, I feel a surge of empowerment, knowing that I am living my message. My book will be raw and unfiltered because my journey—and the journeys of those I hope to inspire—deserve nothing less.

In embracing fear, I have found freedom. And through sharing my story, I hope to empower others to do the same. Let fear be your wingman, not your captor. Stand in your truth, face your fears, and discover the incredible strength within you.

CHAPTER 6

STAGE FOUR FAWNER

In today's world, we often hear about fight-or-flight responses, especially in the context of trauma and healing. These concepts have become buzzwords in modern therapy, representing our instinctive reactions to stress and danger. My journey with therapy, however, has been far more nuanced and deeply personal.

When I decided to pursue couples therapy with my former partner, I recognized the necessity of also engaging in individual therapy. This was my first experience going into therapy with the explicit goal of salvaging my marriage. I had a history of therapy sessions dedicated to healing from my sexual assault, but this was different. This time, the focus was on addressing the intricacies and challenges within our relationship.

Our marriage was floundering, and every effort we made to fix it on our own seemed to worsen the situation. The more we tried to communicate and resolve our issues, the more trauma we inflicted upon each other. Hurtful words were exchanged in moments of pain, and the wounds in our relationship only deepened. I realized that we needed an external perspective—someone who could guide us through this turbulent period with objectivity and expertise.

I remember one day, in a moment of desperation, asking God to help us find the right therapist. For years, I had implored my former spouse to consider therapy, but he had always refused. To him, therapy was unnecessary and an outright NO. Our marriage had reached a critical juncture: either we tried something new, or I would have to leave.

He reluctantly agreed to give therapy a chance. This was a monumental step for us, one that I did not take lightly. I knew that for therapy to be effective, we needed a therapist with whom he felt safe and comfortable. But I was unfamiliar with any therapists in our area, adding another layer of complexity to our search.

Finding the right therapist felt like an overwhelming task. We needed someone who could not only understand our unique dynamic but also navigate the deep-seated issues that had been festering for years. I scoured resources, asked for recommendations, and prayed for guidance.

I did some searching and came up empty-handed. So, I simply said a prayer one day and implored, "God, send me a therapist." Right after that prayer, I was invited to go speak about women's empowerment on a zip-lining tour. A bunch of women piled into the back of an RV Hummer and rode up to the very top of the mountain. Each of us took turns, one at a time, clipping to the zip line and zipping down the mountain. At the bottom, we all huddled around the riverbank where I was to give my presentation about women owning their power. It was a small, intimate group and I didn't know any of the women. I gave them each an opportunity to introduce themselves. One by one they told me who they were and where they were from and shared a little bit about themselves. One lady stood out to me when she said she was a couples therapist and spoke about some of the problems she helped with. I immediately had a clear answer. *This woman is meant to be the therapist you asked God to find.*

After my speech, I pulled her aside privately and asked her if it would be inappropriate, since we had met on this women's retreat, if I asked her to be my professional therapist. She told me she could do it, and not even a week later, she became our couples therapist. The things I have learned from that woman have stayed with me to this day, and some are lessons that I am teaching you in this book.

She was a modern-day angel in my life, and though she didn't save my marriage, she showed me ways to save myself. I have been working with her since 2020 and still to this day she is my therapist.

Early in our couples therapy sessions, our therapist introduced us to a concept that would profoundly impact my understanding of myself and our relationship: fawning. Within the first few months of therapy, after carefully assessing the challenges we faced, she explained how this often-overlooked response was affecting our marriage.

When we think of stress responses, the terms "fight" and "flight" often come to mind. These responses are well-known and frequently discussed in the context of modern-day healing and psychology.

The "fight" response involves becoming aggressive, defending oneself, criticizing, and erecting emotional barriers.

The "flight" response entails withdrawing, running away, hiding, or numbing oneself to escape the source of distress.

Alongside these, "freeze" is another common reaction in which an individual becomes paralyzed, unable to move or make decisions due to overwhelming fear.

However, there is a fourth response that is less commonly discussed but equally significant: fawning.

Fawning is a survival mechanism that involves appeasing and placating others to avoid conflict and ensure safety. This response often manifests in individuals who have experienced prolonged trauma or abuse, leading them to prioritize the needs and emotions of others over their own.

WHAT DOES FAWNING MEAN?

Fawning can be understood as the act of excessively seeking to please or pacify others, often at the expense of one's own needs and well-being. It is a coping mechanism— developed in response to traumatic experiences—in which the individual learns that their safety and survival depend on making others happy and avoiding confrontation. Here are some key characteristics of fawning.

1. **People-pleasing behavior**: Fawners often go to great lengths to make others happy, even if it means neglecting their own needs

and desires. They may constantly seek approval and validation from others, fearing rejection or disapproval.

2. **Suppressing emotions**: To maintain peace and avoid conflict, individuals who fawn may suppress their own emotions and opinions. They might present a façade of contentment and happiness, masking any underlying distress or discomfort.

3. **Avoiding conflict**: Fawners are typically conflict-averse and will do whatever it takes to avoid disagreements or confrontations. This can involve compromising their own values and boundaries to keep others satisfied.

4. **Hyper awareness of others**: Those who fawn are often highly attuned to the emotions and needs of others. They might anticipate others' reactions and modify their own behavior to prevent any negative outcomes.

My therapist observed that I had spent most of my life in a state of fawning. This was a startling realization, as I considered myself an enlightened and self-aware individual. I initially challenged her, thinking she might have concocted this concept. However, as she elaborated on it, I began to recognize how deeply ingrained this behavior was in my life.

In our regular therapy sessions, I came to understand that I was a perpetual fawner. Fawning, as it manifested in my life, looked like living a seemingly high-functioning life filled with happy and excited moments while acting as if nothing was ever wrong. It was my protective coping mechanism I employed when the trauma or pain was so severe that it became incomprehensible. Our therapist pointed out instances in my life where she expected my reaction to be catastrophic or extremely emotional. Instead, I remained cool, calm, collected, and focused. This, she explained, was fawning.

This behavior was not a badge of honor. Instead, it revealed that I was completely dismissing, hiding, and numbing my trauma to the extent that I had created a new reality where the trauma didn't seem to exist. To address this, she guided me through the creation of a trauma timeline—a detailed record of the most traumatic events in my life. Using Eye Movement Desensitization and Reprocessing (EMDR) Therapy, we worked to rewrite those stories and confront the buried emotions.

I initially thought my *first experience* with fawning *began* when I was brutally sexually assaulted at age eighteen. However, through the process of constructing my trauma timeline, I discovered that my propensity to fawn extended much further back into my childhood. This behavior had become a part of me at a very young age.

Fawning, as I learned, was a coping mechanism I adopted because it was modeled by my mother. Growing up, I watched her navigate life's challenges by placating others, smoothing over conflicts, and maintaining an outward appearance of composure and happiness. In many ways, I learned to fawn by emulating her behavior.

For context, let me illustrate what fawning looks like. Imagine enduring a deeply traumatic event, one that should rightfully elicit a profound emotional response. Instead of reacting with the expected levels of distress, you present a façade of normalcy. You might even find moments of joy and excitement amid the chaos. This is not genuine happiness but a survival tactic. It allows you to function in daily life while the underlying trauma remains unaddressed.

Fawning involves appeasing others, suppressing your own needs and emotions to maintain peace and, often, to avoid further harm or conflict. It can be mistaken for resilience or strength, but in reality, it is a form of self-betrayal. Over time, this behavior can erode one's sense of self and lead to a profound disconnection from one's own emotions and needs.

In therapy, I learned to recognize when I was fawning and began the difficult work of breaking this pattern. This involved acknowledging the trauma, allowing myself to feel the associated emotions, and learning to express my needs and boundaries more authentically. It was a challenging process but one that was crucial for my healing and personal growth.

Understanding fawning has been a pivotal aspect of my therapeutic journey. It has allowed me to reconnect with my true self and approach my relationships with greater authenticity and emotional honesty.

THE IMPACT OF FAWNING

While fawning can be an effective short-term strategy for ensuring safety and avoiding harm, it can have significant long-term consequences on an individual's mental and emotional health. Here are some of the ways fawning can impact a person.

1. **Loss of self-identity**: Constantly prioritizing others' needs can lead to a diminished sense of self. Fawners may struggle to identify their own desires, values, and boundaries as their focus is primarily on pleasing others.

2. **Emotional suppression**: By habitually suppressing their emotions, fawners can experience increased anxiety, depression, and emotional numbness. Over time, this can lead to a buildup of unresolved emotional pain.

3. **Relationship challenges**: Fawning can create imbalanced relationships in which the fawner consistently gives while receiving little in return. This dynamic can lead to feelings of resentment, burnout, and isolation in the fawner as well as their partner.

4. **Decreased self-worth**: Relying on external validation for self-worth can be detrimental. Fawners may develop low self-esteem and a lack of confidence in their own abilities and decisions.

In sharing this part of my story, I hope to shed light on the often-overlooked response of fawning and encourage others to explore and address this behavior in their own lives. By doing so, we can move toward a more authentic and fulfilling existence free from the constraints of past traumas and learned coping mechanisms.

Stage Four Fawner

Within the tapestry of my childhood memories, my mother's fawning behavior wove a complex narrative that intertwined acts of kindness with a subtle undercurrent of self-neglect. Her innate desire to please others and alleviate their burdens was evident in every aspect of her being. She would go to great lengths to ensure the comfort and happiness of those around her, often at the expense of her own needs and desires. When I was a child, I admired her unwavering dedication to serving others, believing that her ability to put others first was a sign of unparalleled strength. However, as I matured, I began to see her self-sacrifice and constant need for approval were taking a toll on her well-being. Her fawning, while rooted in a genuine desire to connect and nurture, often led to a pattern of self-suffering and a lack of self-compassion.

Through observing my mother's struggles with setting boundaries and prioritizing her own happiness, I learned a profound lesson about the importance of self-love and self-compassion. I witnessed how her relentless people-pleasing tendencies eroded her sense of self-worth and left her feeling depleted and unfulfilled. It became increasingly clear to me that true strength does not lie in sacrificing your own well-being for the sake of others but rather in finding a balance between caring for yourself and caring for those around you. My mother's fawning, which I once saw as a symbol of strength, revealed itself to be a double-edged sword—a fragile façade of selflessness masking a deeper struggle with self-worth and self-acceptance.

The night of my brutal sexual assault, my parents had rushed to pick me up from the hospital and brought me straight back to their home, causing me to leave behind everything in Southern Utah. In the dead of night, my married siblings also arrived at my parents' home, gathering together in a show of familial solidarity after the harrowing ordeal our family had just endured. We sat together in the living room, tears flowing freely, offering solace through embraces, conversations, and shared silence united in the pain that had befallen us all because of my assault. It was a rare moment, perhaps the only one, where I was allowed to openly express the hurt I felt from my assault.

In the days that followed, however, it seemed as though the assault had been erased from our collective memory. No one, not even my closest friends and family, asked me about the details or pain again. Many casually asked, "are you okay?" but no one truly felt comfortable enough to sit with me in my pain. I don't blame them, though. I wasn't comfortable sitting in my own pain, either. Only three weeks later, I returned to college in Southern Utah as though nothing had happened. My parents and I met with the college Dean and decided I should withdraw from my more demanding classes—anatomy and microbiology—and resign from the dance team. The completion of my spring semester was just six weeks away, and the stress of finals and a rigorous dance schedule seemed daunting. Since more than half of my classes didn't seem as advanced, I jumped back and finished as if I was completely *capable* of finishing the semester. This highlights my consistent fawning response—a coping mechanism in which I minimized my trauma to adapt and survive.

This significant experience set a precedent for how I would handle subsequent traumas in my life. When I discovered my partner's struggle with pornography six months into our relationship, it was treated as inconsequential by him and the one family member I dared to tell. When she said, "My partner looks at it too. It is totally normal for men, unfortunately," I felt totally shut down and hopeless. How could it be otherwise? I had almost lost my life, and within weeks, everyone expected me to be back to normal. From that moment at eighteen, I learned that I had to survive by fawning—pretending everything was okay despite the turmoil inside.

Fawning became a survival strategy that seemed to be a superpower. It allowed me to excel professionally, earn respect in my community, and achieve far more than seemed possible given my personal struggles. People marveled at my resilience, unaware of the internal battles I faced. I appeared unstoppable, earning accolades and accomplishments, all while enduring traumatic experiences that would cripple others. Yet, beneath the façade of success and high achievement, fawning was silently eroding my sense of self-worth and perpetuating harmful patterns.

By age thirty, I had achieved what many would consider remarkable success, yet I realized fawning was not a superpower—it was a disease. It enabled me to function at a high level outwardly while internally struggling with decisions and situations that compromised my well-being.

Fawning, I came to understand, was my kryptonite—a source of strength that ultimately undermined my ability to authentically connect with myself and others. It allowed me to endure immense challenges but at a cost that became increasingly clear over time.

Despite its detrimental effects, fawning taught me resilience and the capacity to persevere through adversity. Recognizing its impact has been pivotal in my journey toward healing and reclaiming my authenticity. Understanding that fawning—once a necessary survival tool—requires unlearning and healing that is essential in rediscovering true empowerment and self-worth.

When my therapist explained fawning and then diagnosed me as a chronic fawner, why I did the things that I did made a lot more sense.

> *Why I accepted the treatment I accepted*
> *Why I was the world's biggest people pleaser*
> *Why I suppressed my emotions*
> *Why I would over apologize*
> *Why I didn't have any boundaries*
> *Why I prioritized my children's and spouse's needs over my own*
> *Why I had no self-care practices*
> *Why I avoided conflict and hid from confrontation*
> *Why I was taking accountability for others' problems*
> *Why I overgave*
> *Why I accepted less*

All of these behaviors were symptoms of fawning. But the true disease lies within: I didn't love myself.

I know that some of the whys listed above might be true for you. And if you are a fawner, you probably want to check out and stop reading this book right now.

Stage Four Fawner

If you feel the need to check your texts, scroll on social media, or yell at a kid . . . stay with me.

You are part of the fawning club, BUT you didn't even know it. Now that you do, you can call back all the power that you have been giving away.

You have everything you need right here, right now, to own your power and accomplish the dreams that you have ignored for the sake of others.

You are stronger than you know.

And you choosing to take accountability for parts of you that are messy means you are ready to step into your power.

My therapist showed me how I had been fawning in my relationship, and how it showed up. I avoided conflict at all costs, putting everyone else's opinions and desires before mine. I had zero boundaries, acting as if I didn't need anything in life except to breathe, and then I would apologize for doing that.

RECOGNIZING AND OVERCOMING FAWNING

Acknowledging and addressing fawning behavior is crucial for personal growth and healing. Here are some steps that can help in overcoming this survival response.

1. **Self-awareness**: The first step is recognizing when you are engaging in fawning behavior. Pay attention to situations when you feel compelled to please others or avoid conflict at all costs.

2. **Self-compassion**: Understand that fawning is a learned response developed to protect you. Approach this realization with kindness and compassion rather than self-criticism.

3. **Therapeutic support**: Working with a therapist can be incredibly beneficial in addressing the root causes of fawning and developing healthier coping mechanisms. Therapeutic approaches like EMDR (Eye Movement Desensitization and Reprocessing) can be particularly effective.

4. **Setting boundaries**: Practice setting and maintaining healthy boundaries in your relationships. This involves clearly communicating your needs and values and not compromising them to appease others.

5. **Building self-worth**: Focus on activities and practices that boost your self-esteem and reinforce your sense of self-worth. This can include self-care routines, hobbies, and affirmations.

One of the biggest parts of my fawning was suppressing my emotions. I had no knowledge of how to express how I felt when I was upset. My therapist made it very clear that fawning is an absolute disease, and I was at stage four. So, what did this mean in my relationships? How did I stop fawning?

What was the first step I took?

CHAPTER 7

THE CHALK LINE IN THE DIRT

My pathway out of fawning started with boundaries. This was the answer I was seeking.

Boundaries are like fences. Imagine you buy a piece of land out in the middle of nowhere. Close your eyes and imagine what it looks like. Once you have pictured it, open your eyes and keep reading. This is not a time for a quick nap. Boundaries are crucial to learn.

Now, imagine the house on the land. Is it a small cottage, brick home, cave, apartment, RV, condo, or mansion? Whatever it is, it's yours and now you have to maintain it, keep it clean, tidy, and ultimately SAFE. This is your home. Your haven. Your protected place. This is where you raise your babies, sit on the porch with your lover, watch sunsets, cook meals, and look at the stars. *This is your sanctuary.*

Imagine your home. How does it feel? Secure? Peaceful? Sacred?

How would it make you feel if someone opened your front door without knocking, walked in, went into the kitchen, opened the fridge, took out your food, and started eating it at your kitchen table?

That would be incredibly intrusive. Bold. Dangerous.

Maybe instead, someone walked into your yard and without even realizing it was your land, threw a blanket down and set up a picnic.

Less offensive? Maybe an honest mistake, but still not okay that they came into your yard where your babies play.

You have to build some sort of boundary around your land so people know the difference between your house and the next-door neighbor's.

You need to let people know where your property line is.

This is essential so that people don't just come meandering onto your land.

People may encroach on your space and start building their home too closely to yours if you haven't established where your land ends and theirs starts.

Marking where your safe place starts and ends **is a boundary.**

Making a clear line of where your neighbor's grass starts and yours ends is a boundary.

The Chalk Line in the Dirt

Some people's boundaries are white picket fences. Some people's boundaries are a chalk line in the dirt. Some are a half pony wall, four foot concrete pillars, or a barbed wire fence.

I want you to imagine what your boundaries look like. Are they so small and insignificant, like a chalk line in the dirt, that people don't even see them? Are they like an old rickety fence that barely stands up on its own? Maybe your boundary fence is ten feet high with no entrance in or out.

As I kept doing therapy, I became aware that my boundaries in life were nothing more than lines in the dirt. And no one could see or respect that. I had no fences around my safe place. There was no way to distinguish what was mine or let others know they were trespassing into my world.

I was willingly letting people come in and out, and that meant I was totally open and vulnerable to being hurt and threatened. People were metaphorically building *their* homes on *my* property. People were taking over my yard. People were walking into my home and claiming it as their own.

I started working on learning how to set boundaries, and before I knew it, my boundary of a chalk line in the dirt became a twelve-inch-tall fence. *I was starting to set boundaries!* I had built a fence that could only keep out a small dog, but nonetheless, this was a huge improvement. I was finally having insight on what boundaries were important to me and, piece by piece, I had a fence and a list of "do nots." This list was a specific chart of things I would no longer allow in my life. It was encouraging to see I had finally *built* boundaries, but people could still easily step over my fence and walk into my home unannounced. Even though I had built a small fence, **I was not enforcing my boundaries, and I was allowing people to walk over the fence, push open the front door, and come on in.**

THE FENCE OF BOUNDARIES DOES NOTHING IF YOU ALLOW PEOPLE TO CLIMB OVER AND ENTER *ANYWAY*.

The more my therapist gave me courage to build boundaries, the bigger my walls got. She then pointed out it doesn't matter how big I start setting my boundaries—if I have a front gate that's wide open, people will still walk through. I was learning that not only did I have little to no boundaries set but I also allowed people to walk over them all the time.

This manifested in this practical example: I would share with my partner that I did not feel comfortable with him looking at pornography. If he had the desire or slipped up and looked at it again, I would request he tell me about it. That was my boundary, and time and time again, I would find pornography that he was concealing from me. He continued to break my boundary, but here's the thing: I never did anything about it. The boundary should have been, "if you continue to look at pornography without disclosing it to me, I will . . ." I never followed through with enforcing my boundary with him.

Though I never had a consequence for people who broke my boundaries, there was still an improvement because now I at least had a fence.

My next step in learning boundaries was policing people from coming in and out of my gate. As I became stronger, more confident, and more aware that I was a boundaryless woman, I could see the other relationships in my life where I was getting walked all over.

I had longtime friends who mistreated me because I had never set boundaries.

I had family members disrespecting me because there was no fence to keep them out.

It manifested mostly in my marriage, where I was allowing behavior that was not okay simply because of my lack of boundaries and enforcement. I realized that when I didn't enforce my boundaries, I couldn't be upset. When someone walked into my house and burglarized it, it was because I hadn't set up a fence.

Next on this journey, my therapist had me write down everything I could possibly think of that I needed to set boundaries on.

This meant setting standards with my partner's addictions and what I would and would not allow.

This meant writing down scenarios that, if my friend crossed that boundary again, I would have to stop hanging out with her.

This meant acknowledging that no matter how much I loved my family, if they kept doing certain hurtful things, I would have to distance myself from them.

Boundary work was really hard for me. It essentially meant, "Now I have a set of rules, and if you break them, there will be a consequence." Setting the boundaries was the beginning; enforcing them was the part I kept failing at. As a people pleaser, I felt bad executing my boundaries. It was as if my safe, white house on the prairie now had a beautiful picket fence, but when someone came plowing through my yard, ripping down my fence with their car, I would walk out and say, "Oh, don't worry. It's no big deal." I didn't hold them accountable for the damage they just did to my property. That is the perfect scenario of being a people pleaser, which is equivalent to fawning.

Fawning is the blanket of suppression, and the three components that manifested the most for me were people-pleasing, having no boundaries, and suppressing my emotions.

You would have had no idea if I was depressed, anxious, or suicidal because I fawned and acted as if I was happy. You could back your car into my car on purpose, and *I would say sorry*!

Once I learned how to get a hold of my people-pleasing, set boundaries, and express myself, guess what happened? I no longer fawned. I learned how to cure my disease. But things happen when you're miraculously cured of a plaguing disease. You look at life a little differently. Now, my relationships didn't look the same because I wasn't going to take s*** anymore.

All of a sudden, I stopped texting the friend who took private things I shared with her and told others, and that caused a lot of problems.

All of a sudden, I stood up for myself and set a new boundary with a family member who constantly criticized how I parented my kids, and that caused a lot of problems.

All of a sudden, when my partner crossed my boundaries on what I would accept in our relationship and did the one thing I asked him not to, I realized I have a f****** problem.

No one had ever seen this version of Robyn.

To be honest, I hadn't either, and it was really scary.

I remember a family member distinctly telling me I had changed, that my heart was cold, and that I was different. She said this the first time I challenged her for saying something inappropriate about how I choose to parent my children. Cold-hearted? No. I had actually just spoken the truth. But it looked as if I was having a rapid change in who I was because **I was no longer pleasing people.** I was choosing to not be abused.

A friend told me, "You've changed." She didn't mean it in a nice way. By telling me this, she was acknowledging that my growth meant I had changed and that was uncomfortable *for her.*

Setting boundaries means you have to change. People may see you as rude, direct, stern, or even "different." But that is necessary to stop fawning.

If I could go back in time and talk to my twenty-five-year-old self, I would tell myself that it takes great humility to continually challenge and re-examine your own beliefs and stories to see if you might find something more true. No belief or story is final. Everything you think and believe now will change. Embrace it. It's good. Lean into it. I see the comment "you've changed" as one of the hugest forms of flattery. Change equals growth, and I'm really proud of myself for allowing change.

In a world where you and I are anomalies, rare in our essence, we must confront the lingering fear that resides within us. Picture that you rise above the planet and observe the multitude of silenced women, those forced into submission, those who know no other way than to fawn or take to the streets. What do they need? They need to have an understanding of why we've softened our truth—a survival mechanism ingrained in us. But what if our life's barometer wasn't merely to survive but to thrive?

As women, we've been conditioned to make everything soft, to round the corners of our truth, hoping to be heard while absorbing the accountability of everyone around us. Who decided when and how we should speak the genuine truth? Does that trace back to our mothers, their mothers, or even a heavenly mother? The truth, softened and absorbed, manifests as fear, a cancer that infiltrates our very beings. The cure, it seems, lies in teaching people to love themselves.

Fawning is the fear of accepting that you are not enough. We fawn to survive because we believe that without appeasing others, we won't be accepted. This behavior stems from a deep-seated fear of inadequacy and rejection. We fawn because we feel powerless and unable to win the battle for self-worth on our own terms. It feels safer to please others than to step into the ring and face potential rejection or failure. The perceived loss of self-esteem and acceptance seems so much greater if we were to confront these fears head-on and potentially fail. Therefore, fawning becomes a survival mechanism to avoid the pain of perceived inadequacy and maintain a semblance of acceptance, even if it means sacrificing our true selves.

The generation of women before us fawned. We have always been silenced and will continue to be silenced until we speak our boundaries and hold them as truth.

Setting boundaries is not an act of selfishness but a fundamental aspect of self-care and emotional well-being. It teaches others how to treat you and lays the groundwork for relationships that are balanced and fair. When you communicate your boundaries clearly and consistently, you reduce the likelihood of misunderstandings and conflicts. Enforcing your boundaries demonstrates your commitment to your own values and needs, reinforcing your sense of self-worth.

Remember that boundaries can evolve. As you grow and change, so, too, can your limits and expectations. This adaptability is crucial because it allows you to navigate different stages of life and relationships with confidence and clarity. By giving yourself permission to speak your truth, you also encourage others to do the same, fostering an environment of honesty and openness.

The capacity to set and enforce boundaries, coupled with the courage to speak the truth, empowers you to build a life filled with respect, integrity, and genuine connections. This not only benefits you but also inspires those around you to honor their own boundaries and truths, creating a ripple effect of healthy, respectful relationships.

You have the capacity to set boundaries, defining what is acceptable and what is not in your relationships.

You have the strength to enforce these boundaries, ensuring that others respect your limits and understand your needs.

You have permission to stop softening the truth and speak your mind openly and honestly without fear of judgment or rejection.

Embracing this power allows you to create healthier, more authentic connections with others, where mutual respect and understanding thrive. In doing so, you also model for those around you, especially your children, the importance of self-respect and personal autonomy.

CHAPTER 8

ACCOUNTABILITY IS OUR RESPONSIBILITY

It is easy to see where our partners, parents, and church are in the wrong, and probably because they DID do something to validate that response from us.

We don't usually go around making up stories of people yelling at us, hurting us, or treating us with neglect. We experience them because they are real for us.

Seeing these actions is easy.

The hard part is knowing what we need to do and then doing it. We need to get real with our own accountability and OWN our responsibility in the mess.

The truth is, we are as much the monsters in the acceptance of the behavior as the person who is doing it.

If someone hits you more than once—*you let them.* You accepted their behavior.

If someone yelled at you and you didn't stand up for yourself, that means *you allowed it.*

We are staying, which proves we accept their behavior.

This becomes how we cope with less than what we deserve. In fact, we create an entire world and ecosystem, **to accept less and become less.**

Fawning keeps us alive in this unsafe ecosystem, to the point that we adapt to survive.

By accepting and fawning we are creating a huge monster that has a million legs . . . *aka all of our friends and family.*

It was hard for me to accept I was a part of the problem. But after deep healing work and guidance from my therapist, it became very clear. I needed to take more radical accountability for why my marriage really ended.

Maybe it was less about all these traumatic things happening and me being abused. Perhaps it was just that the abuse was normal from the beginning and became the standard of my relationship.

But the real truth was, **I was the abuser of my own life.**

This truth shook me. Because this concept destroyed all of my beliefs. I mean, I had experienced thirteen years of abuse. Right?

This new concept rocked me . . . what if my former partner wasn't the villain?

What if the abuse occurred because *I allowed it?*

And then it hit me.

> *Abuse happened **because** I settled.*
> *Abuse happened because I accepted less.*
> *I abused myself.*

I now know my power, my capabilities, and how beautiful and strong I am.

I now know and **own** my godliness.

I didn't know these things when I was twenty years old and newly married. I had never been able to see my worth, so I 100% settled in my relationship. I settled in a lot of things because I didn't think I was worth anything better.

Over the years, I began to see my worth. I started to value myself. And this completely contradicted the life I had willingly agreed to. This contradiction is why I kept feeling a pull in my soul—a pull for something different. And not just different but **something greater.**

Who I was when I got married was a broken twenty-year-old. I had been through severe sexual assault and kept pretending life was going great. Ignoring the truth of the pain that was stuck inside of me weakened my ability to see my worth.

For a very long time, I blamed my previous partner for our marriage ending. He did ignore me, neglect me, and treat me poorly. But, there is so much more to this story.

You see, there are always different stories about the same experience. In one person's eyes I was the victim. In another's I was the victor. Same story, different perspectives.

I realized I could spin this whole thing and say that I'd been abused and I escaped. Or, I could see the abuse as simply being with someone who didn't see my power. The abuse can simply be that I was living below my potential.

So, why did I get divorced? Abuse literally lived in my day-to-day life because I was compliant about the things I allowed him to do. The way he talked to me, the way he neglected me—that's abuse.

I took it. I allowed it. And by allowing it, I allowed him to do it more frequently and at more severe levels. That's on me.

Was there abuse and neglect from my partner? Yes, emotional and eventually physical. But I left the relationship because I finally realized who the true abuser was.

It was me. I had allowed the abuse. I had shackled myself.

I was my abuser. And I had to own up to that.

The narrative needs to be switched that it's not necessarily the men who keep abusing us; it's our compliance in fucking letting them do it.

We stay. We take the hit.

We lie there and let it happen.

I stayed in a relationship that suffocated me. That is self-abuse.

Our relationship wasn't great, but it wasn't always horrible. We got along, but we were more like roommates who would momentarily connect and then go on living our own individual lives. From the outside, you would have classified us as "happy," a normal, average couple.

I wish I would have been given permission to leave my relationship based on the sole fact that it was just basic.

I wish someone would have validated my feelings early on when I knew this was not a relationship that stimulated growth.

I wish I hadn't been led to believe that "marriage is hard," and you stick it out no matter what.

The societal narrative often glorifies endurance and resilience in marriage, implying that unless there are extreme circumstances, you should remain committed. This mindset traps many in relationships that are fundamentally unfulfilling and stifling.

Where is the woman who encourages and celebrates you for realizing it's time to leave, simply because you are being suffocated? Simply because you can't grow in this ecosystem? It feels like we are only allowed to leave for BIG THINGS—abuse, infidelity, addiction. These are indeed valid reasons to end a relationship, but why can't we just leave *because we know we shouldn't stay?*

The culture of enduring hardship at all costs does a disservice to personal growth and happiness. It neglects the subtle yet profound ways in which a relationship can inhibit one's potential. The inability to thrive emotionally, intellectually, or spiritually within a relationship is a significant issue, one that deserves acknowledgment and respect. Relationships should be spaces where both individuals can flourish, where mutual growth is encouraged and celebrated. When this is not the case, it's perfectly valid to consider leaving.

It's crucial to cultivate an environment where women feel empowered to make decisions based on their well-being and personal development. We need voices that normalize the idea that personal fulfillment and happiness are legitimate reasons to end a relationship. This perspective honors the importance of self-awareness and the courage it takes to act on that awareness.

Encouraging women to trust their intuition and validate their feelings can lead to healthier, more fulfilling lives. It's time to challenge the notion that staying in a subpar relationship is a badge of honor. Instead, we should celebrate the bravery it takes to recognize when a relationship is no longer serving its purpose and to take steps toward finding relationships that fulfill and encourage self growth.

In essence, leaving a relationship because it is basic or unstimulating is an act of self-respect and an acknowledgment of one's worth. It's about choosing a path that fosters growth, joy, and fulfillment. We must shift the dialogue to support and uplift those who make such decisions, understanding that the pursuit of a vibrant, thriving life is reason enough to move on.

The time is now. And I'm that woman celebrating you and encouraging you to take that step toward a vibrant life.

This book is a testament to my journey, not a reflection of a former partner's actions. He does not deserve that acknowledgment. This is about me finally waking up after thirty years and hoping to inspire others to awaken and learn these lessons sooner:

You are not obligated to endure mistreatment for the sake of love. Never allow anyone to diminish your worth or make you feel small.

Do not tolerate being shoved around or slapped across the face, physically or emotionally. You deserve respect, not pain.

Refuse to stay in a relationship with someone who constantly puts you last and treats you like an afterthought. You are not an option. You are a priority.

You are not made for scraps when you are the whole damn feast. Demand more than the bare minimum because you are worthy of abundance and love.

It's time to honor yourself and let go of anything or anyone that doesn't recognize your value. You deserve to be cherished and celebrated, not merely tolerated.

This journey is about claiming your power and living authentically. Do not settle for less than what you deserve. Stand tall and own your worth.

Do not allow yourself to be gaslighted into believing that enduring abuse or disrespect is a measure of strength. True strength is knowing when to walk away.

You are not responsible for anyone else's happiness at the expense of your own. Prioritize your well-being and refuse to be guilted into staying in a toxic situation.

It is not selfish to prioritize your own needs and desires. Self-care is essential, and you have every right to put yourself first.

You are not defined by your past or by the people who tried to break you. You are defined by your resilience, your courage, and your unwavering commitment to your own growth and happiness.

Do not settle for a partner who prioritizes their family of origin over you. You deserve to be cherished and respected as their chosen life partner. A marriage is about creating a new family unit, and your needs and feelings should come first in your spouse's life.

This is your life, and you are the author of your own story. Do not let anyone else write your narrative or dictate your worth. Take control, make bold choices, and live authentically.

You are a force to be reckoned with. Do not dim your light for anyone. Shine brightly and unapologetically, knowing that you deserve all the love, respect, and joy the world has to offer.

And most importantly...

Sweetie, you can leave simply because you know you shouldn't stay. You don't need another reason—a big story or a bruise on your cheek. You get to leave simply because you have the knowingness inside to do so.

CHAPTER 9

BREAKING FREE

Many of us believe we can't leave. Our mothers stayed. Their mothers stayed. The belief is that you stay. No matter how poor your life is, even if you are ignored, mocked, yelled at, loved only for sex ... **you stay**. But, this belief has run its course.

This belief ends now.

Just as in 1954 when running a sub-four-minute mile seemed like an impossible feat, until it wasn't. Did you know that before 1954, scientists and physicians believed that if you were to run a sub-four-minute mile, your heart would explode and your lungs would collapse? People were afraid to even attempt this goal. It was considered dangerous and deadly.

For decades, the quest to break the four-minute mile captivated athletes and the public alike. Many believed it was a physiological and physical barrier that couldn't be breached; running a mile in less than four minutes was considered beyond the limits of human capability. The record for the mile stood at 4 minutes 1.4 seconds, set by Swedish runner Gunder Hägg in 1945, and later matched by John Landy of Australia.

Roger Bannister, a British middle-distance runner, etched his name into history on May 6, 1954, when he became the first person to run a mile in under four minutes. This achievement marked a monumental milestone in athletics and human endurance, shattering a barrier that had long been deemed insurmountable.

In 1954, at age twenty-five, Bannister made his historic attempt at breaking the four-minute mark on the track at Oxford's Iffley Road Stadium. The conditions were less than ideal, with blustery winds and intermittent rain threatening to foil his endeavor. Nonetheless, supported by fellow runners Chris Chataway and Chris Brasher, Bannister took to the starting line with determination and focus.

As the race unfolded, Bannister settled into a brisk pace, meticulously tracking his speed and conserving energy for the critical final lap. With Chataway and Brasher pacing him admirably through the early laps, Bannister surged ahead in the last lap, propelled by sheer willpower and the roar of the crowd.

In a dramatic finish, Bannister crossed the finish line in 3 minutes 59.4 seconds, achieving what was once deemed impossible—a sub-four-minute mile. His feat electrified the world of athletics and captured the imagination of millions, proving that with perseverance, meticulous preparation, and a steadfast belief in one's abilities, monumental goals can be achieved.

Bannister's achievement transcended mere athletics; it became a symbol of human potential and the relentless pursuit of excellence. His record-breaking run not only inspired generations of runners but also underscored the power of determination and courage in the face of daunting challenges.

According to Wikipedia, as of June 2024, this four-minute barrier has been broken by 1,869 athletes.

All it took to break the belief was one man proving he could run a sub-four mile.

All it took for the other 1,868 athletes to do something that was once considered impossible was the belief that it could be done.

Navigating the tumultuous waters of divorce, I faced the daunting prospect of being forced to sell my new home—a sanctuary that encapsulated my life's journey and provided solace in times of turmoil. Witnessing others in similar situations and hearing their stories, I was inundated with messages of inevitability: divorce often meant selling the marital home and splitting the assets.

My resolve to defy this fate grew stronger with each passing day. As conversations about my divorce unfolded with friends and family, I boldly asserted, "I will find a way to stay." Despite skeptical half smiles and well-meaning nods of disbelief, I clung to the hope of staying in my sanctuary.

However, reality struck hard when my father gently intervened, imparting the harsh truth that relinquishing the home might be inevitable. Even my lawyer, with unwavering confidence from years of practice, confirmed the prevailing precedent: marital homes of the same scale as mine were typically sold.

She told me that in her twenty-five years of practice, she had never had a client stay in a home of my size. She assured me that even if I could find a way to not have to sell it initially, I would have to prove to the court that I could afford to stay in it. I remember looking her directly in the eyes and saying, "You have never met Robyn Williams. I will stay in my home. I will defy your odds and everyone else's. You are about to meet the first single mother to figure out how to keep her house and afford to stay."

I bet she didn't really believe me.

But that didn't matter because I BELIEVED ME. I was her first client to not only stay in the marital home and afford it but be granted full ownership of and equity in said home in the decree.

Against all odds, I defied expectations. Through grit and resourcefulness, I navigated the complexities of mortgage payments, bills, and sustaining my lifestyle on a single income. It was not without its challenges—I worked tirelessly, unearthed solutions I had never previously imagined, and embraced a level of resilience that surpassed even my own expectations.

To this day, the logistical miracle of retaining my home remains a testament to perseverance and self-belief. It was not merely about retaining property but about reclaiming my autonomy and proving the depths of my resilience. In the midst of adversity, I found empowerment in standing tall, facing down doubts, and forging a path that defied conventional wisdom.

This echoes a resounding affirmation:

> *Belief in oneself can move mountains.*
> *Belief in oneself can keep homes.*
> *Belief in oneself can break physical barriers.*

All it takes is one person to believe in themselves to break years of "truth."

All it takes is one woman to break the belief that you must stay in unhealthy relationships.

One...

If you don't know one, then let me be the one who shatters that belief. I left a marriage after thirteen years and having birthed four kids. No one thought I could stay and pay for our $1.8 million house on my own. I had sold my profitable business just two years before the divorce, a business that would have supported me fully had I still owned it. I had recently started three small businesses with $0.00 of reported income, and I was a single mom of four with no steady income and no real plan. I had recently left organized religion, so I was doing this without a community circled around me. I did not have a "trust fund" father or anyone I could ask to borrow money from.

I had every reason stacked against me staying in my home. But my heart told me otherwise.

On paper I had NOTHING to prove I could stay in my home.

But I had belief deep in my soul. And that was enough.

I am not telling you to get divorced or leave religion. No. I am telling you that you can shatter the belief that says you *have to stay* in any relationship or religion that is unhealthy or abusive in any way.

By authentically sharing our stories, we alter the narrative and give every woman the courage to do the same.

Let's challenge the beliefs that hold us hostage. Let's rip out the pages of our books that say we HAVE to be something other than what we *want* to be. And then, let's fill those books with the chapters that we have been compelled to omit.

Imagine a book that is filled with blank pages, urging women to write the words they've kept hidden, to share their untold stories.

This book would be a place to read each other's stories and witness the collective bravery.

This is the book I'm speaking of. The one you're reading right now.

Remember back in Chapter 5 the invitation I extended for you to fill the blank pages at the end of this book with your untold stories? I want you to write your chapters—the hidden ones, the stories you've kept deep inside. This will be a collaborative journey that breaks generational trauma. Write your stories on the blank pages, then pass this book along to another woman so this book will become a torch of light illuminating the way for others. Together, we will liberate ourselves from the fear of sharing the raw, unfiltered truth.

Every woman has unique fears, which may include the fears of not being loved, accepted, or enough. Owning these fears and being unapologetically authentic is liberating. Fear no longer controls me. The liberation of being unafraid and speaking the truth is worth any price.

Owning fear is accepting it and allowing it to coexist with you rather than fighting it outright. Instead of rejecting it, let fear sleep beside you. Ignoring fear creates an illusion of safety, which is a toxic pattern. Breaking free from such toxic patterns requires acknowledging the fear and finding worth beyond these cycles.

Fear tells the truth about our insecurities and anxieties. Breaking free involves sharing these fears openly despite the discomfort. Living in fear is living a lie; the key is to break through and speak the truth even when you're scared. **Fear isn't the liar. The real lie is pretending fear isn't there.**

The desire for justice and liberation is often stifled by fear. Fear is the authority that silences us, keeps us from sharing what we should. This book is a commitment to 100% truth, challenging readers to face uncomfortable topics. It's a call to stop accepting incomplete versions and embrace the bravery of being the one who speaks up. The fear will no longer rule. It's time to write the stories that have been suppressed for far too long.

Now, as I declare, "Fear, I call the shots now!" I take control, write my book, and make choices without being governed by anyone else's fear. Fear is already in my bed, and I'm choosing to now make love with it.

But it wasn't always this way. Fear seduced me to cover up other people's sins.

Reflecting on my former partner's issues and my fear of facing reality, I acknowledge my role in protecting him from natural consequences. How often do we think we are saving someone from their own sins, yet we are robbing them of their accountability? When we don't allow natural consequences, we are stealing their opportunities to grow and change. Protecting them may seem noble but is really fraudulent. You do not get to cover up someone's sin to lessen the blow to them. You are stealing their growth. What is the greater sin? Allowing someone to feel and experience their consequences, or taking those consequences on as your own?

Despite facing my deepest fears, I've embraced the liberation from fear. It's a paradox—hating my life while having the best life ever. I find strength in being the one making love with fear and still having a good time.

There is power in reclaiming my truth, accepting the consequences of potential repercussion, and YET being unafraid. I've played my part, confronted my fears, and I am ready to face whatever comes next, liberating myself from the shackles of fear.

I call on you to open your eyes and face fear.

I call on you to sit with it long enough that you no longer feel scared.

I call on you to not allow fear to linger in your bed any longer.

Embrace the discomfort and challenge it head-on, understanding that fear loses its power when confronted.

Recognize that fear is often just a shadow cast by our own insecurities and uncertainties.

By acknowledging and confronting it, you reclaim your power and allow courage to take root.

Let your heart be the compass that guides you through the darkness, knowing that you have the strength to navigate any obstacle.

Allow this journey to be a testament to your resilience and determination.

No longer let fear dictate your actions or your dreams.

Stand tall, breathe deeply, and take that first step forward, for it is in facing our fears that we truly find our freedom.

CHAPTER 10

BETTER THAN NOTHING

"It is better than nothing." How many times have we heard this phrase whispered like a mantra echoing through the corridors of our minds, urging us to settle for less than we deserve?

How many times have we convinced ourselves that staying in a deadened state of comfort is preferable to venturing into the unknown where growth and fulfillment await?

But what if we dared to challenge this notion? What if we refused to accept mediocrity as our fate and instead chose to pursue our dreams and desires with unwavering determination?

Is it truly better to remain stagnant, to accept mediocrity as our fate, than to strive for something more?

Is it truly better to sacrifice our dreams, desires, and sense of self-worth for the sake of maintaining the status quo?

The women before us—our predecessors and foremothers—may have believed so. They may have taught us, both through their words and actions, that settling for "better than nothing" was the path of least resistance, the path of least pain, and that sacrifice and self-denial were the price we must pay for a semblance of comfort and security. But in doing so, they unwittingly perpetuated a cycle of self-denial and self-betrayal—a cycle that we, as modern women, have the power to break.

One of the most insidious lies we've been taught is that we cannot be alone—that we must settle for companionship, even if it means sacrificing our autonomy and self-respect. But the truth is, being alone is not synonymous with being lonely. Solitude can be a source of strength, empowerment, and self-discovery. It is better to be alone and true to ourselves than to be in a relationship that stifles our growth and suffocates our spirit.

Are we not worthy of a better lover, more attention, or deeper intimacy? We've been conditioned to believe that we must settle for crumbs of affection rather than demand the love and respect we deserve. But the truth is, we are worthy of love in its fullest expression. We are worthy of being cherished, adored, and valued for who we are, not just for what we can offer.

We are worthy of partners who see us for who we truly are and cherish us accordingly.

Similarly, we've been taught to blame ourselves for the actions of others, to believe that we are somehow responsible for their mistreatment or neglect of us. But the truth is, we are not to blame for the shortcomings of others. We are not responsible for their choices or behavior. We are worthy of love and respect, regardless of how others may treat us.

We've been led to believe that we are not capable of making money, providing for ourselves, or pursuing our own passions and ambitions. That we are not capable of achieving greatness. That we must settle for a life of quiet resignation and unfulfilled potential.

We are capable of achieving greatness beyond our wildest dreams.

We are capable of financial independence, professional success, and personal fulfillment.

We are capable of rewriting the narrative of our lives and creating our own destinies.

We are capable of pursuing our passions and ambitions with courage and determination, forging our own paths to success and fulfillment.

We've been told that mediocre sex is better than nothing—that we should settle for physical intimacy devoid of passion, connection, and pleasure. But the truth is, we deserve so much more than that. We deserve to experience love in its most passionate and fulfilling form. We deserve to be with partners who ignite our desires, cherish our bodies, and honor our boundaries and consent. We deserve to be ravished, to be engulfed in passion. We deserve to experience life in all its richness and depth—to savor moments of joy, passion, and connection that ignite our souls and fill us with a sense of purpose and fulfillment.

It is time to cast aside the lies that have held us captive for far too long. We have to embrace the truths that empower us, that liberate us, that set us free. It's time to dare to believe in our own worth, our own potential, our own capacity for love and fulfillment. Rather than settling for "better than nothing," the best thing we can do for ourselves is to embrace the infinite possibilities that await us when we dare to dream, to hope, and to believe in ourselves.

We are the architects of our own destinies, the captains of our own ships. We have the power to shape our lives according to our own desires and aspirations. We have the power to break free from the chains of self-doubt and self-limitation and to step boldly into the bright future that awaits us.

So today, and together, we no longer stay for something that is merely slightly better than NOTHING.

Say it out loud.

NOTHING? I AM ACCEPTING SOMETHING ONE NOTCH BETTER THAN NOTHING?!

No! We will not accept "nothing"! We will not accept "sorta." We will not accept "okay." We will *rise* and only accept fullness, greatness, and liberation. You are worth more than "nothing."

Let us rise, my sisters, and claim our rightful place in the world.

Together, let us build a community of support and encouragement, where every woman's voice is heard and valued. Let us celebrate each other's successes and uplift one another in times of struggle. By standing united, we can dismantle the barriers that have historically kept us from reaching our full potential.

It is time to redefine what it means to be a woman in this world. Let us rewrite the narratives that have confined us and create new stories of empowerment, resilience, and triumph. Let us be bold in our ambitions, unapologetic in our desires, and relentless in our pursuits of greatness.

We have the power to transform our lives and in doing so inspire future generations to follow in our footsteps. Let us lead by example, showing the world that women are not just capable but exceptional.

Our journey may not be easy, but it will be worth every step. Together, we can *RISE* above the ordinary and achieve the extraordinary.

CHAPTER 11

THE CHAINS WERE NEVER LOCKED

Be accountable for your own slavery. History tends to repeat itself until someone takes accountability for their own enslavement. This applies not only to historical events but also personal situations, like feeling enslaved in a relationship.

As the echoes of victimhood resounded, I found myself questioning the essence of enslavement. Was I truly a victim, or had I willingly borne the shackles, wearing the role of "slave" in my relationship as a badge of honor? I realized there is a fine line between genuine victimhood and self-imposed enslavement.

For years I allowed myself to believe that I was trapped in my relationship, bound by invisible chains forged from societal expectations, religious beliefs, and my own insecurities. I blamed my partner for my unhappiness, convinced that he held the key to my freedom. But in reality, the chains were never locked; I held the power to break free all along.

It began with a subtle realization that my actions were driven by a deep-seated belief that my worth was tied to how much I could do for others. I would go out of my way to anticipate my partner's needs, often neglecting my own in the process. This behavior left me feeling drained and resentful, but I couldn't understand why.

As I confronted the root cause, I realized that I was trapped in a cycle of self-imposed victimhood. I believed that if I could just do enough for my partner, he would finally see and appreciate me. However, this belief was flawed from the start, as true appreciation should come from within, not from external sources.

With this newfound awareness, I made a conscious decision to empower myself. I began setting boundaries and communicating my needs openly and honestly. I stopped waiting for my partner to validate me and instead focused on validating myself.

Through this process, I learned the importance of self-love and self-appreciation. I realized that my worth was not contingent on how much I could do for others but on how much I valued myself. I started practicing self-care and prioritizing my own well-being, knowing that only by loving myself could I truly love others.

As I embraced empowerment, I found liberation from the self-imposed chains of victimhood. I no longer felt the need to prove my worth through my actions. Instead, I embraced my inherent value as a human being.

It wasn't until I took a hard look in the mirror and acknowledged my role in perpetuating my own enslavement that I began to see a way out. I realized that I had willingly surrendered my agency, allowing fear and complacency to dictate my actions. I had convinced myself that I was powerless to change my circumstances, when in fact I was the one holding the key to my liberation.

Breaking free from the chains of self-imposed enslavement required courage, self-reflection, and a willingness to take accountability for my own actions. I had to confront the uncomfortable truth that I had been complicit in my own suffering and only I had the power to break myself free.

Reflecting on personal experiences, the importance of accountability became clear. A therapist once challenged me to accept accountability even when dealing with difficult situations, like dealing with someone who seemed beyond reason. By acknowledging my own role in the dynamics and reclaiming ownership, I found the power to initiate change.

It wasn't easy. There were moments of doubt, fear, and uncertainty, but with each step forward I reclaimed a piece of myself that I had long forgotten. I rediscovered my strength, my worth, and my inherent right to live a life of freedom and fulfillment.

I realized that true liberation begins within. It's about taking ownership of our choices, refusing to be defined by our past, and embracing the boundless potential that lies within each of us. It's about recognizing that we are the architects of our own destinies and that no one else has the power to enslave us unless we allow it.

As I stand here today, no longer shackled by the chains of my past, I am filled with a sense of empowerment and gratitude. I am grateful for the lessons I learned, the obstacles I overcame, and the freedom that has come from taking accountability for my own enslavement.

I invite you to join me in breaking free from the chains that bind us. Let us reclaim our power, our agency, and our right to live a life of joy, purpose, and fulfillment. The chains were never locked. It's time to set ourselves free.

SO HOW? HOW CAN WE SET OURSELVES FREE FROM OUR OWN SLAVERY?

1. **Acknowledge the unlocked chains.**

    First, we must peer down at our feet, and acknowledge that the chains were never truly locked. We have been choosing to remain bound by them. It's time to awaken to the power of accountability, a word that takes empowerment to the next level.

2. **Embrace personal accountability.**

    We have to insist on embracing accountability for our own shackles. No one else locked us in. If there's a key, we're the ones holding it. It's time to step out and take responsibility for where fear, doubt, and anxiety have been controlling our lives.

3. **Shift your perspective.**

   It's become a competition for women, a race to see who's suffered the most. But it's time for a shift in perspective. Instead of boasting about our pain, let's focus on accountability and healing.

4. **Turn away from negativity.**

   We have to turn away from negative conversations and gossip. Instead, let's embrace a culture of solutions, problem-solving, and mutual growth. This positive environment emerges through personal growth and breaking down toxic patterns.

5. **Direct energy toward self-love and creation.**

   There are parallels between where we direct our energy and what we attract. Let's shift our focus to self-love and creation. If we dwell in self-hate, we'll attract negativity, but by focusing on positivity and growth, we invite positive outcomes into our lives.

6. **Overcome distractions and addictions.**

   Distractions can *be* addictions. True healing comes from taking full accountability for our lives. It's about recognizing and overcoming our addictions to become whole. Accountability is the key to breaking free from destructive patterns.

7. **Recognize generational impact.**

   Our children feel our fears, absorbing our unresolved traumas. It's vital to recognize how our wounds can impact future generations. It's time to break free from this cycle, to heal ourselves so that we can create a brighter future for our children.

Let us carry these lessons forward, knowing that each step we take toward healing and growth is a powerful statement of our strength and resilience.

We are not defined by our past or our pain; *we are defined by our capacity to rise above and shine brightly.*

Together, let us embrace our journey and inspire others to do the same, creating a legacy of empowerment and transformation for ourselves and future generations.

CHAPTER 12

RAGE IS THE CATALYST

Imagine a pot of water simmering on the stove, gradually heating up until it reaches a boiling point. For many women, this pot symbolizes their romantic relationships, where tensions simmer beneath the surface, occasionally reaching a rolling boil before subsiding once more. However, it is rage that serves as the catalyst, the proverbial salt that instantaneously brings the water to a rolling boil.

When I reflect on my past relationship, I'm reminded of an old parable about a pot of water and a lobster. As a child, I learned that if you gradually heat the water with the lobster already inside, it won't notice the temperature rising until it's too late. The lobster stays, unaware it's being cooked alive. But if you were to put the lobster directly into boiling water, it would instinctively jump out to save itself.

In my former relationship, I found myself slowly acclimating to rising temperatures, unaware of the toxicity gradually engulfing me. Looking back, no one willingly plunges into scalding water. Yet, the water wasn't boiling from the beginning—it began as cold, and little by little it heated up.

By the time the water reached a rolling boil, it was clear that staying meant risking my well-being. Why did I endure this? Initially, I didn't realize the harm. When the simmer escalated to a boil, I panicked, ready to leave. But just as swiftly, it would return to a simmer. Comforted by familiarity, I convinced myself to stay—it was my home, my ecosystem, although uncomfortably hot and unhealthy.

There were moments of happiness amid the turmoil—joy, peace, and excitement—but deep down, I knew I shouldn't be there. Each time the heat escalated to a rolling boil, instinct told me to leave, yet each time it subsided, I hesitated, swayed by well-meaning advice and the comfort of the familiar.

Living in simmering water became the norm, even though it was far too hot and toxic. I found solace there, even as I understood the water would be healthier elsewhere. It took the trauma of those boiling moments to stir me into action—to recognize that staying in this environment was unsustainable.

The rage I felt during those boiling points finally spurred me to action, forcing me to confront reality and liberate myself from the unhealthy cycle.

> *Sacred rage is the fuel for changing your life.*
> *Sacred rage is what changes the world.*

Rage is not evil. It is only evil when used to cause hurt. But this same energy can be the fuel for CHANGE.

Let the rage that you feel from being mistreated be the fuel that helps you get out.

Use the rage of things being unfair BE the fuel for JUSTICE.

Rage can be blinding when we don't listen to it. Rage blinds us when we choose to not take action.

But rage can also be the thing that finally saves you. The rage doesn't just show up. Rage doesn't just appear. If your life is working, rage isn't a visitor. Actually, you won't feel it at all.

Rage comes when there is something not in alignment. Rage is the truth coming to you to wake you up.

Don't ignore it. Don't shame it.

Rage will finally meet you when you are ready to say no. I felt anger a lot in my relationship, but it was not enough for me to take lasting action. When rage finally entered me, it was a barometer. Once rage came into me, I could not turn back, and that's how I knew when it was time to move forward with real plans to exit the relationship. Anger wasn't enough for me; all it did was remind me of the problems. But when rage came, it was a sign from God that I was finally ready. I finally found the energetic capacity inside me to stop the abuse.

In my own experience, rage served as the breaking point in my relationship. Like many women, I endured the ebb and flow of emotional temperature, becoming accustomed to the constant simmer of discontent. Yet, it was rage that ultimately propelled me into action, shattering the status quo and forcing me to confront the toxicity of my relationship.

While rage may initially evoke feelings of fear or uncertainty, it ultimately serves as a catalyst for empowerment and transformation. Like the proverbial salt in a pot of water, it has the power to bring long-standing grievances to a boiling point and ignite a fire within us, propelling us toward action and liberation and prompting us to confront and address the underlying issues in our lives. By embracing rage and harnessing its transformative power, women can reclaim agency over their lives, forging paths toward healing, self-discovery, and fulfillment.

Have you found yourself experiencing these thoughts?

> *I am losing out on so much of my life because I don't want to look at what really is.*
> *I don't want to do the work to feel or to fix my relationship.*
> *I know that once the work starts, my relationship could end.*

I knew that last statement in my former relationship. I knew the second we started going to couples therapy, the second we brought these things to the table, it could go two ways. I was going to work my ass off to save my relationship, but deep down, I feared it would be the start of the end.

So, I felt safer staying in mediocre, staying within my pot of water that was always too hot but bearable. And honestly, I got used to it.

Stop living in mediocrity because you are robbing yourself of experiencing life at a level you don't yet know is possible.

One of the questions I get asked the most in regard to divorce is, "When did you know it was time to leave?" I had many moments that any woman would say *should* have been the time to leave. When I knew it was time to leave was not the first time I was betrayed; it was not the first time something traumatic happened; it was not the first time I ever had the awareness that the relationship was toxic; it was not the first time I was ever lied to.

When I finally knew it was time to leave was when I was finally tired of getting boiled in my own relationship. I made the choice, "I don't want to be fucking burnt anymore."

When women reach out to me about divorce, the thing I hear most frequently is, "I want validation to know when I should leave my marriage." And I tell them, "The timing is right when you're ready to validate yourself." That's it. It's the right timing when **you don't need anyone else's acceptance of your choices**, when you don't need your dad to tell you you can leave, when you don't need your best friend to say that it's time.

It's when you're finally ready to validate yourself and say, "I'm not doing this anymore, and I trust me in my decisions. I give myself permission to leave. I validate myself." That's so fucking powerful. And when you get there, it's because you walk through rage to be able to have that power.

I don't know that I've ever seen a woman who is enraged like a woman who finally knows it's time to go. They have walked to the top of the mountain and there is no way they're coming back down the same path. They will walk through sagebrush and trudge their own goddamn weed-whacking path before they ever go back the way they came.

The trust in your own validation is when you know it's time to go. I'll never tell a woman it's when he cheats on you, it's when he lies to you, it's when he has an addiction. No, it does not matter what the event is. When you decide to validate and trust yourself, you will know.

Rage says, "No fucking more."

For you, the result of this rage may clearly say that you have to leave your marriage. Or it may look like you stay in your marriage but it will finally have improvements because you say "no more." Your rage is the thing that pushes you and your partner to do the healing work to have the shifts. Rage doesn't mean you have to burn the whole fucking town down. It just means it is time to make the changes.

Rage says, "This will NOT happen ANYMORE!"

Sacred rage is a potent force for transformation. It is the catalyst that can ignite personal and societal change. This powerful emotion, when channeled constructively, can be the driving force for positive change. Let the anger and frustration from being mistreated fuel your journey toward freedom and justice. Use the intense energy of righteous indignation as a beacon for creating a fairer and more just world. By harnessing sacred rage, we can turn our deepest pain into a force for profound change and growth.

CHAPTER 13

YOU CAN FIGURE IT OUT

There will be women reading this book that resonate with the mistreatment happening in their lives, but their logic will trump their hearts. They will say things like:

> *Why should I leave?*
> *How can I leave?*
> *I truly don't want to leave because my life is handed to me on a silver platter.*

I get it, ladies. I was there with you. When I left my marriage, I lived in a brand new, $1.8 million house. Prior to my divorce, I had just sold my successful business and was enjoying being a stay at home mom while starting a few passion projects on the side. My partner made good money and I did not *have* to work, though I chose to be an entrepreneur. That just brought me joy, and I had no pressure to bring the dollars in.

I got to stay home with my babies 24-7, go to lunch whenever I wanted, and buy most anything I felt we ever needed or desired. I rarely had a care in the world when it came to money. When I would go to buy

Christmas or birthday presents or book a vacation, I didn't even have a thought on how much money I could spend. That felt nice, that financial freedom, though I traded it for the slavery of my heart. Literally, I was free as a bird when it came to my logistics, my finances, where I lived, and how I could travel, but I was shackled to the core. My heart, my soul were shackled.

I had to get frank with myself.

> *Am I going to live below the capacity in my soul but above the financial standard of the average human? I'm spoiled rotten.*
>
> *Do I give up this human experience to have a Godly one?*
>
> *Do I trade in my mansion on earth to build mansions in other women's hearts?*
>
> *Do I give up my bank account—the account that is constantly filled with money—to feel joy in unindebted currency?*

The answer is yes. It took me a long time, and ultimately, the only way I was finally able to give up my carefree lifestyle to take a risk on feeling more joy, was that I found self-love.

Maybe you've woken up, but you've still got to take action. What are you going to do with your awakened state? Again, do you tell your girlfriends you're unhappy and then go home and sleep with him so that you can live in that same house? You are actually living as a prostitute in your own life when you decide that you would rather take a comfortable lifestyle over truly listening to your heart. You are a soul prostitute, and I can tell you that because I did the same thing.

I sold my soul for a beautiful home. I sold my soul for a complacent marriage. I literally was a prostitute in my own life, and a prostitute is a slave. In exchange for luxury, I had sex with a man I knew was keeping me below my potential. In exchange for worldly comfort, I had sex with a man I knew didn't love me at the capacity I deserved love. I had sex with a man I knew lied to my face because I also lied to myself about my true desires.

I was a prostitute.

When you awaken to the truth, it's not enough to simply acknowledge it; action must follow. It's like finally opening your eyes and realizing the chains that once held you were never locked—you were simply sitting there, bound by your own fears and insecurities. Staying in a situation where you're unhappy, merely for the sake of comfort or familiarity, is akin to prostituting your soul. It's exchanging your true desires and potential for a complacent existence.

I was that person. I traded my dreams and self-worth for a beautiful house and a stable yet hollow marriage. I stayed in a relationship where I knew I was undervalued, where I settled for crumbs instead of demanding the feast I deserved. I was complicit in my own entrapment, telling myself that the comfort of the known was better than the fear of the unknown.

If these words resonate with you, then know that your own rebellion is on the horizon. Rage, the raw and powerful emotion that pushes us to break free, will visit you. It's not about guilt or shame if you're not ready to leave yet—many of us stayed in those situations for far too long. But when rage comes, let it be your catalyst for change. Let it propel you out of the chains that bind you, and do not allow yourself to step into another form of slavery, even if it seems less oppressive.

You will need to find your own way, to build your own life from the ground up. You'll have to learn to make decisions, earn your own money, and rebuild the confidence that was stripped from you. I know you can find solutions that right now don't even seem possible. I know you will find the way to make the money you need to feed your children. I know you will be able to manage the drama and the climax of leaving a relationship. I know it will be hard. I've been there. But you can do it.

I know you will have moments when you truly believe you made the wrong decision. I know because even though I left my relationship, I went back several times. Even when I knew I was being enslaved, I walked back with my wrists up and said, "Shackle me. I'm more comfortable here." Numerous times after leaving my relationship and filing for divorce, I walked back and said, "I've changed my mind. Here are my wrists." I had to do that f****** hard thing over and over and over again until I decided, *I'm not a slave, and I am prolonging my pain by going back when I **know** I'm not supposed to stay here.* It would have been ten times easier to love myself enough that when I left the first time, I did not look back.

The path won't be easy, and at times it will feel lonely. People may not support you, and some might even criticize you for choosing freedom over comfort. But remember, their fear of leaving their own self-imposed chains doesn't have to be yours.

Embrace the challenge, the pain, and the uncertainty. For on the other side lies the joy, peace, and clarity that only true freedom can bring. You are capable of enduring hard things and emerging stronger. As you journey through this transformation, know that you are not alone, and that every step you take toward your liberation is a testament to your strength and resilience.

Believe in yourself. Your journey is your own, and it is valid. Walk the path, even if it's just you. For in walking it, you are not only breaking your own chains but also lighting the way for others who are watching and waiting for their own moment of courage. You are powerful beyond measure, and your story of breaking free will be the beacon of hope for those still in the darkness.

I'm so proud of you. I am so proud of you that you're going to finally believe you deserve a better life. I am so proud of myself that I left. I am so proud of the women who have gone before me who never get their stories told, who will never be heard from in a book. I am proud of you, and I see you. I am proud of the women who will come after us who decide they are not going to be slaves in their own lives anymore and will help other women find freedom. I am proud of you. It will not be easy, but I know you can do it because you're reading this book and you're ready to break the bonds of your self-imposed slavery.

Rising: *Fearless Women Rebelling*

I know this is hard to hear, but I know you are capable of doing hard things.

I have a quick message for you here.

Rise Check In:

Write out 10 things from the last decade that you've done well, that are epic, that you're proud of.

1. _____
   _____
   _____

2. _____
   _____
   _____

3. _____
   _____
   _____

4. _____
_____
_____

5. _____
_____
_____

6. _____
_____
_____

7. _____
_____
_____

8. _____
_____
_____

9. _____
_____
_____

10. _____
_____
_____

Believe in your strength and resilience, for within you lies the power to break free, create your own path, and inspire others to do the same.

CHAPTER 14

THE BROKEN PIECES

After the long and devastating journey of my divorce, I found myself needing a way to celebrate the end of that chapter and reclaim my joy. In a spontaneous and light hearted moment, I turned to a quirky ritual I had become known for on Instagram: dancing in oven mitts worn as boots. This playful act had once been a symbol of my free spirit and creativity, a way to bring laughter and joy to others. However, throughout the painful process of my divorce, my spirit had been so broken that I hadn't danced in my "oven mitt boots" for over a year.

The day I finally decided to put them on again felt monumental. It was a declaration of my resilience and a celebration of reclaiming my identity. As I turned on the music and pressed record, my heart felt lighter, and for the first time in a long while, I truly felt free.

As I took that first step, my foot snapped under the weight of the moment. The pain was palpable, and the process of healing seemed daunting. Little did I know, this fracture held a lesson in resilience.

During a consultation with the foot doctor, I was introduced to an enlightening concept: bones, when healed properly, become stronger than they were before the break. This notion challenged my assumptions about the aftermath of fractures—not just in bones, but in life itself. As I pondered the parallel between the physical and emotional fractures in my life, a powerful realization emerged. While my former relationship had left me broken in many ways, it also offered an opportunity for newfound strength and growth.

In the dance of healing, both physically and emotionally, I embraced the idea that the broken parts of me were not condemned to eternal weakness. Instead, like my foot, the bones fused stronger together in their mending. I, too, had the potential to grow stronger in the places where life had fractured my spirit. Paradoxically, a sense of gratitude seeped in for the things my former relationship had broken within me. In acknowledging the pain, I found a deeper appreciation for the strength that had evolved in those vulnerable spaces. The fractures became the catalyst for an unexpected journey toward resilience and self-discovery.

The foot doctor's advice lingered: healing must be done correctly to build strength. Similarly, my emotional recovery required deliberate self-care and introspection. The broken pieces of my spirit needed to be delicately reassembled, ensuring a stronger, more resilient me. As I stand at this crossroads of reflection, I realize that the dance between brokenness and strength is an intricate choreography of life. The fractures, whether physical or emotional, are not merely scars; they are testaments to the resilience of the human spirit. From the brokenness, a stronger self can emerge, ready to dance anew in the rhythm of life.

Remember, when you break, it is an opportunity to grow stronger than before. Take the time to heal correctly, so your fractured heart and spirit can mend and become more robust. Brokenness is not a weakness; it is a call to rise and step into the strength awaiting you. Brokenness is where we RISE.

CHAPTER 15

SELF-LOVE

Would you be surprised to know I used to hate myself? It's true. For most of my adult life, I was crippled with deep feelings of unhappiness towards myself. I want to share my journey from self-hate to self-love. I need to stress the importance of understanding what self-love truly is, how to achieve it, and what it is NOT. Being cruel to ourselves is a learned behavior, not something that is inherent. Look at our children for example. When they are young, they don't make comments about how ugly or stupid they are. They love themselves fully. Self hate is a learned behavior we see others emulate, then do so ourselves. When we focus on self-love, it frees up mental energy, allowing us to pursue more significant goals.

The journey through self-discovery brought me to a profound revelation: self-love is the key to liberation. I realized that my actions for others were, in essence, a yearning to fill a void within myself. The transformative power of self-love became a beacon guiding me toward my true authenticity.

Often, we know what needs to be done. We feel it in our bodies and hear it in our hearts. However, in our self-abandonment and self-neglect, we push aside the truth within ourselves at the expense of our health, joy, and wholeness. Learning to betray ourselves becomes a language we understand because we have been betrayed so often. This cycle of betrayal holds *us* hostage, just as much it does those who betray us.

Self-love resides in listening—listening to what our bodies ask, to the whispers of truth inside our hearts and then honoring them. Self-love isn't about commercialized trips to the spa or shopping sprees. It is the love we pour into ourselves, listening and responding to our own needs.

If you have been in any form of abuse, it likely occurred when your needs were ignored. Abuse was most painful when you asked for support and were met with blank stares and deaf ears. In turn, ignoring our own needs turns us into our own abusers. We inherit a roadmap of life from those who raised us. Often, they were taught to ignore their own needs and live in self-neglect, and they consequently passed down the opposite of love.

Self-abandonment and neglect were the stepping stones of our lives and were so often used as badges of honor. We watched our mothers ignore their needs, and they passed down the opposite of love. They gave us their own trauma *and* the trauma of the women who came before them. This was the energetic "hope chest" filled with generations of shit, pain, and abuse.

The "hope chest" ends here. Burn the chest and commit to never passing it down again. Rise as the powerful woman who never neglects herself again, who loves all of herself.

You may not be ready to give up your current lifestyle, and that's fine. But you must step into radical accountability and own the fact that you're your own abuser. If you're not ready to leave an enslaving relationship, acknowledge that you don't love yourself yet. Accept that you're willingly keeping the shackles on. Only leave when you have fallen in love with yourself. If you enslave yourself and stay, be open and honest about it.

That's hard to read, but if you're ready to be unshackled, I'm absolutely going to show you the way.

HOW I FOUND SELF-LOVE

Self-love is not a verb. It's not an action word. It is not a series of activities. Self-love is not taking yourself to the spa, meditating, going to the mountains, or lunching with friends. Those are *acts of self-care*, not self-love. Self-love is knowing you are enough, confident that you have everything inside you to create the life you dream of. Self-love is a tangible energy that others can see and feel. Self-love is not what you do. Self-love is what you *are*.

I have had so many people in the last year tell me they have never seen me happier. They literally see a tangible glow coming off of my body and even permeating through their phones. I do not tell them it's because I left my marriage. I do not tell them this happiness they're seeing, that

Rising: Fearless Women Rebelling

they can touch, came because I left the Mormon church. It is 100% because I learned to love myself. Self-love is tangible, and when you walk past or interact with someone who loves themselves, it will rub off on you.

You will feel it. You might not be able to keep it because you don't love yourself, but it is so tangible that you can see and feel it. Self-love cannot be something that you read about in a book and then you just have it. You cannot achieve self-love from a self-help book. You can only *become* self-love by embodying love. If you are love, you are self-love. If you are love, you love others. If you are love, you spread love. If you are love, you see love. And if you are love, you attract love. If you want to love others, you have to love yourself first. If you want your children to find someone later in life to love, you better f****** make sure you teach them to love themselves. If you are not the example of self-love for your children, they may find themselves in a situation later on decreasing their chances of finding a healthy relationship.

They may get into a relationship out of desperation, just as I did. My mother did not love herself, nor did her mom before her love *herself*. I have empathy and understanding as to why my mother couldn't teach me self-love and why that put me in a situation where I fell for desperation. I do not have hard feelings toward my mother, but I have an expectation for myself that *not* teaching self-love ends with me. I will teach my children self-love because I truly love myself.

It's not a foolproof plan that when they get older they will find an incredible relationship and never have the problems that I'm all talking about in this book. But their chances of *avoiding* deceit, lies, and betrayals increase. Their chances of calling in self-hate—like I called in everything I thought about myself—their chances of low self-confidence, being walked all over and abused decrease. Because I abused myself, I did not love myself. If I had been a woman at twenty years old—a child at twenty years old—who had actually truly loved herself, I energetically wouldn't have even surrounded myself with the person I married.

You better believe I am trying my very hardest to exemplify self-love to my children so they have a better chance at setting themselves up for success in love. Is it really hard to get to? Yes. And you're probably thinking, "This sounds like a shiny little trinket, but how does one actually obtain it?" It's very simple. When you think about loving your child, what do you have to do to love that human? You have to have empathy. Your kid makes a lot of mistakes. They can have moments that are annoying, but you still love them. So, you have to have empathy for yourself. I've had to have empathy for the bad decisions I've made. I have to have empathy for not handling my divorce like I should have. I have to have empathy for getting myself in a situation at twenty years old that, on paper, was logistically stupid.

Empathy for yourself is essential. Love yourself unconditionally, as you would love your child. Rewrite your beliefs about yourself. Start with self-care. Self-care acts as drops that fill the jar of self-love. Embody the care and take radical accountability for your imperfections.

Another piece of self-love—the piece that's left out the most—is taking radical accountability for your darkness. Take radical accountability for the parts of you that you don't love, the parts of you that are a little bit of a mess, the parts of you that aren't perfect.

Accept and love *all* parts of yourself, even the messy ones. Do not stay in relationships that hinder self-love. Acknowledge your generational trauma and work on it. You cannot achieve self-love without confronting and accepting your trauma.

When you become radically accountable with acknowledging that you are imperfect and have parts of you that are messy, and you can still love and accept those parts, you can love yourself. That's why I am challenging you to not stay in relationships that you know are not right because you cannot love yourself when you're not willing to accept parts of you. That's why I am asking you to look deeper within and find your generational trauma.

If you can't look at your trauma, you're not going to accept it. You have to be able to put it on the table before you eat it. If you want to embody self-love, you've got to look at the s*** no one wants to look at. You've got to own that part of the reason your marriage is failing is your fault. You've got to be okay knowing that some of the relationships that feel really toxic are toxic because you're in them, and you still have to love yourself anyway. Once you can do that, self-love will start flowing through you. Self-care is the action verb step.

It is okay if you stayed in a marriage for twenty years and you knew you needed to leave. It's okay if every time you look in the mirror you call yourself ugly. It's okay that when you lose your temper with your children, you hate yourself for it. It's okay that you told a white lie

Self-Love

because it felt safer. You do not have to be perfect to love yourself, but you do have to accept these parts of you and be willing to work on them. You have to be able to give grace and empathy to yourself. Why is it we are so kind and forgiving to everybody else but not ourselves?

If a neighbor were to come into my home, tip over my most beautiful candle and shatter it leaving wax everywhere, I wouldn't meet her with harshness, saying, "Get out of my house! You're never welcome again. Why did you do that to my stuff?" Instead, I would be soft with her, saying, "No worries, no problem; accidents happen." But when *I* do something in my life, even just having a negative thought, I beat myself up about everything. That's conditional love. I was unconditional to my neighbor and conditional to myself.

I was born and raised in Utah, which is known for its snow. Despite this, I have always disliked snow and prefer the warmth of Southern Utah. Honestly, I have to store energetic "acorns" during the summer to live through the winter. I only still live where it's cold in the winter because I have a divorce decree that keeps me here. Otherwise, I would not live here.

I love the red rocks, which is why I wrote this book in Sedona, Arizona. Southern Utah, with its beautiful red rocks, has always pulled me in. It's interesting because my life's biggest moments have happened in Southern Utah. That's where I was sexually assaulted, right in the red rocks. Also, the man that I love more than anything is from Southern Utah, where the red rocks are.

It is a place of significant personal history and growth.

As I wrote my book in Sedona, I was surrounded by a bowl of stunning red rocks. Every morning, I woke up, looked out the windows, and admired how beautiful it was. One morning, I woke up to a rarity: it had snowed in Sedona. Locals told us it was very rare for this to happen. When I saw a fourth of an inch of snow sticking on the nearby mountains, I gasped in disbelief. Giddy, I ran around the house taking videos with my phone. I hate snow, so why did it make me so excited to see it in Arizona? Simply because it was a rarity.

Reflecting on this analogy of the red rocks and snow, it dawned on me that I had abused myself by allowing myself to be with somebody who didn't see me as a rarity. He didn't see me as the powerhouse, witty, funny, energetic, attractive, magnetic woman that I know I am. But here's the thing: how could I ever expect a man to think that of me when I didn't see it myself? The second I learned how to love myself and could see the gifts God gave to me was the second I realized I needed to be in a relationship that honored what a rarity I am. You have to love yourself first before you ask someone else to. Then, make sure you're with a person who can match that love you have for yourself. Once I realized my capacity to love myself, I realized I had the capacity to love my companion at that same level. This meant I had to do a hard diagnostic on my former relationship and see that this person could not match the level that I loved myself.

Now, I am in a relationship with a man I dub the love of my life, and he meets me where I am. He loves me as much as I love me. And I love him as much as he loves himself. I think I am incredible just as much as I think he is incredible. I see him as a gift, and know I, too, am his gift. It

Self-Love

will never work if you're in a relationship with someone and you EACH don't think highly of yourselves.

When I found my fiance, he truly loved himself. He thought he was a gift. He thought he was incredible. So, he had the capacity of the love that he gave to himself to share with me. And I could match that capacity because I loved myself too. This means we can love each other to a tenfold degree.

Reflecting on my past, I realized I had allowed myself to be with someone who did not see my worth because I did not see it myself. Learning to love myself made me recognize my need for a relationship that honors my rarity. I now have a partner who matches my self-love, and that allows us to love each other deeply.

Self-love is the foundation of a fulfilling life. It requires empathy, unconditional love, and radical accountability. It is the key to freeing ourselves from self-imposed limitations and leading others to do the same. Embrace self-love, and rise as the powerful, self-loving individual you are meant to be.

CHAPTER 16

THE INVITATION

There were four potty words in my home growing up: shit, damn, hell, and . . . SEX. I was raised in a devout Christian family—I guess, if you call Mormons "Christians"—and *sex* was not a table topic in my home. In fact, it was not a topic we ever spoke about. It was an off limits, don't ask situation. When *sex* was spoken, the word was charged with energetic vibes of being dirty, gross, and wrong. So it makes sense that I cannot recall my parents giving me the birds and the bees talk. Truly, sex was a topic that was absolutely avoided. We were taught our anatomical body parts were named the "vuh-jayjay," and the "dingle dong."

I remember trying to piece it together in junior high when I found myself in typical teen conversations. Sarah would mention something she heard from a friend. Heather would tell about something she learned from an older sister. I'm not sure if they'd had the birds and the bees conversation, but as the collective, we were uniformly curious. I truly don't know how I escaped teenhood and got well into college and never saw a penis—not even a sketch in an anatomy book. Either my book randomly had it ripped out or that lesson was skipped over.

I never walked in on my parents. I never had a friend who was having sex and sharing her stories. I truly didn't recall having any sexual education growing up. Outside of having little to no sex ed, the narrative around it was that it was bad. Sex was BAD! You shouldn't have it or you wouldn't go to heaven. You shouldn't have it or you would get pregnant. You shouldn't have it or you wouldn't be worthy to enter the temple. You shouldn't have it because a man wouldn't want "chewed gum" (we were actually told having sex would make us as undesirable to men as chewed gum). I was taught and shown the way that sex was a demon and any sexual desires we had should be hidden and shamed. I did not even know I was a sexual being.

I remember journaling about my first "orgasm" when I was nineteen years old. I was making out with a kid I was dating at the time and I felt him get an erection. We were fully clothed and not even passionately kissing. The hardness I felt happened to be in the exact spot at the exact moment and BOTTA BING BOTTA BOOM—you know the drill. I had my first orgasm. I had no idea what it was. No one had ever told me what one was, let alone described the sensations or protocol. I went home and wrote about it in my journal and it's as hilarious as it is just so sad.

I remember thinking it was bad that I had been turned on by kissing (like duh, hello! Isn't that the point?). I felt so bad about how this specific kissing session sent me into this "freeze up" moment that I went and told my local bishop (church leader) about it months later as I was preparing to marry and enter the temple.

Bear with me for a moment on this tangent, but why did a sweet little twenty-year-old go and explain in detail to a local bishop—who was also her neighbor—her sexual "freeze up" story? It makes me barf when I think about it—how I shared, in explicit detail with him, what had happened and how I felt that because it did happen, I may not be able to get married in the temple in a few months. Why did I feel that my body's natural instinct of pleasure was a sin I needed to confess? I should have gone to my mom or sisters, but we did not have a relationship that supported any topics like sex. And because I'd had my little "make out freeze moment," I now felt unworthy to enter into the temple. Remember, we were *fully dressed* and *just* kissing!

To make a long story short, I was absolutely sexually suppressed and had zero education about my own sensual and reproductive abilities. I was never even educated on what "jizz" was until my last year of college when a group of boys made up a funny rap with that word in it. Later that night I had to privately Google search what it meant.

This felt even more conflicting when I married at the age of twenty and LOVED SEX right out of the gate. I was a little surprised to realize I understood the mechanics of it all because I previously had no idea, but I figured it out really quickly. Sex was something I enjoyed and I never got tired of. This is especially surprising considering my sexual repression and lack of education growing up.

After I got married, the topic of sex remained taboo. None of my friends, family, or neighbors ever really talked about it. I had to learn all about sex through my own education of trying this and that. I really enjoyed figuring it all out with my partner and we had a good sex life. I'm surprised that even though I had little to no exposure to body positivity when I was a child and teen, I figured out sex so quickly. I'm surprised I didn't struggle more in my early days of learning sex.

As I started having kids and finding friends who were more on my authenticity level, *sex* started to become a much less polarized word. The more I shared my experiences with close friends, the less I felt weird talking about it. I was also learning through the experiences my friends shared about with me and discovered I had a "better than average" sex life. I found it surprising how many of my friends were hardly ever having orgasms. Some could count on one hand how many times they'd had one in their entire lifetime. This really bothered me because I was having orgasms most of the time.

I decided I really wanted to be a safe person for women to talk to, learn from, become educated by, and feel comfortable with talking about sex. Before I knew it, I became the local "sex guru" and friends and family were privately coming to me to seek sex advice or ask questions. They struggled with sex. They didn't love it. They never wanted it. They didn't feel comfortable in their own skin. Many of them said it felt like a chore. Most of them said they were doing it to please their husbands. And I learned that many of them were rarely, if ever, having orgasms. This broke my heart. I held it as a really big compliment that they talked to me because, like them, I didn't have a person to talk to about sex. It's funny to think back now because I had no PHD in sex, no masters in anatomy. But these women would come to me and ask how they could improve their sex lives, if "this was normal," and ask about the latest toys.

I'm passionate about making *sex* NOT be a taboo topic anymore, especially to our children. But more importantly, I hope to make *sex* not only *not taboo* but actually CHAMPIONED. I love sex. I love my body. I love my sensual side. It's soft and it's fierce. It's hot and it's gentle. It's erotic and it's spiritual. I want to see our youth receive more education on sex. I want the narrative to change from it's "bad" to *it's sacred*. I teach my children that sex is amazing. And they will love having it. And it feels good. And it's the most beautiful thing they will do . . . but it is sacred.

Sex was one of my former partner's and my strengths and a deep-rooted reason we stayed together so long. We heard other couples struggled with sex so we figured we must be pretty lucky to not have those problems. When things were difficult in our marriage and we really got close to calling it quits, we would always rely on "we have a better-than-most sex life, and that is rare, so we better not give this up." This was a big reason I stayed in this relationship when I was unhappy—I truly felt I would likely never find good sex again. I knew the grass wasn't greener and was willing to trade the possibility of better communication with someone else for good sex in my relationship with my former partner. But what I didn't realize was that the "good sex" I thought I had been having for years was just level one. It was just a ceiling. Though I can honor the great sex life I had with my former partner, I was about to unleash levels of my sensual side I never even knew existed.

From a young age, most girls are taught to cover themselves, hide their beauty, and play small. We are told to "be the good girl," "be quiet," and most importantly, "don't rock any boats."

The invitation for you as a woman is to be so bright that nothing can hide you.

Be so bold that nothing can cover you.

Be heard.

Be seen.

And be the boat that rocks the whole fucking ocean.

We don't do this with our force. We don't do this by pushing our way forward.

Instead, we use the power of the invitation.

This is found within our sensuality.

When a woman owns her power in her sensuality, she commands a room just by breathing. Her presence alone attracts what she desires. And her confidence in herself is the partner in her liberation.

This is when a woman truly RISES. When a woman unapologetically owns her magic, her beauty, and her sensuality, it is inevitable that she will rise.

I've found that the greatest secret to incredible sex is not who your partner is, the size of the penis, or the level of experience. The greatest sex you will find comes when you love yourself and surrender to your pure sensuality.

If you want more orgasms, if you want to have a high sex drive, if you want to learn how to feel your own pleasure—I cannot be your sex guru. The best advice I can give you is to truly find and start cultivating self-love and you will ignite the goddess inside of you that will naturally guide you into your sensual and erotic self.

Finding self-love elevated my sex life in ways I can't describe.

I know you have the power to awaken your sensual self.

Your body knows what to do. If you listen to it, and follow it, you will awaken your sensuality.

If you are willing to do the work and explore self-love, you will enjoy your sensual side and feel liberated from the insecurities you once had.

Orgasms happen when you can relax into pleasure. Do not expect them if you're crippled with self-hate.

Wanting and loving sex is not dirty or wrong. You were created to want it. Don't continue the suppression of your godliness.

CHAPTER 17

INTUITION

Intuition. It is your most important gift. When I think of intuition, I visualize a golden orb inside of me that's celestial and godlike. I believe intuition is a divine gift from God. It's one of the last aspects of ourselves that remains untouched by the limitations of our mortal bodies. Our intuition resides in the spiritual core of our being, connecting us to the Divine. Despite this innate connection, it's often suppressed or dismissed, especially within certain religious teachings. In the religion I was raised in, there was a clear message: don't trust your intuition.

We only rely on this thing called *faith* and nothing trumps faith, not even science, not even logic.

It's just faith.

So, I quickly learned to shut down the part of me that felt godlike, the part that could sense things beyond the grasp of my physical body. Despite my mortal body sensing the impending danger of being assaulted by that man on the trail, I couldn't fully comprehend it. My intuition was clear: this man was going to attack me. Yet, my body refused to acknowledge it.

I could hear myself arguing with my intuition. The thoughts that were running through my mind were, *Robyn, it's in the middle of the day. There's people around, like, there's no way this will happen.*

These thoughts were battling against my intuition.

I've had countless experiences when my intuition feels directly connected to God. It's like I instantly receive these divine pings. However, I was also taught in church to sever that connection, ignore my feelings, and seek guidance from a bishop or someone else first to receive guidance, counsel, or forgiveness. It wasn't until I left organized religion that I realized I didn't need to outsource anymore. I realized that I truly have everything I need within my intuition and direct connection to God. Intuition is the direct line in which I can speak to and hear God. Intuition is my soul.

When women realize this, it won't matter what religion they are in, what their economic status is, whether they're single or married, or if they feel competent or not. Once they recognize they have that connection, they can start honing it, and it will only grow stronger with time.

When I'm aware of that connection, I feel unstoppable. There's nothing I can't do. Fear and anxiety still arise—I'm only human—but they occur less frequently, and I can easily dismiss them. **I affirm my power and reject those negative emotions.**

Empowerment, with its emphasis on *power*, becomes palpable. It's akin to the way men in the church I grew up in experience the priesthood—it's tangible, celebrated, and deeply felt.

It's simply the power of God that is accessible to women as well. Every woman in the room possesses this same power, yet we've been conditioned to doubt it, suppress it, and rely on others for guidance and authority.

We've been instructed to outsource our power at every turn—not just within religion but in various aspects of life. We've been conditioned to believe that others hold the key to our spiritual fulfillment and even forgiveness.

In moments when others might doubt me, I stand firm knowing that I don't need anyone to lead me. I'll chart my own course, with or without their support.

I'll find my own way, whether you're with me or not. This doesn't faze me. Now, I use this power within me to give my children blessings, and call forth powerful prayers, and connect to God. I have never doubted the presence of God within me.

If I truly believe that I'm made in the likeness of God, then there's a part of me that's inherently godly. That's how I tap into my power and intuition.

I bless my children without the formalities of the priesthood—no laying on of hands or anything. *I'm not mocking anything here.* But when it comes to knowing exactly what my kids need at the start of each school year, as their mother, I am in tune and can bless them with what they need. I call it "a mother's prayer." Once I embraced this power and understood how it's intertwined with my intuition, everything fell into place.

Women have been suppressed through religion and society and have outsourced their power. When we allow that suppression to continue, we crack ourselves open to let fear and anxiety crawl back in and fill that space.

Every woman has the ability to be safe. If a situation arises where a man or predator has bad intentions, they're less likely to target a woman who is confident, self-aware, and able to assert herself.

Most of these experiences start with some level of connection, but if a woman can say no and not be a people pleaser, she can often control or even prevent the situation. **Trusting your intuition is key.**

Once you start trusting your intuition, it affects every aspect of life—parenting, dating, even how you interact with family. When I learned to trust myself and speak from my heart, it was a transformative experience. For much of my life, I was told to be quiet, to hold back, and that it wasn't proper or "within my power" to express myself fully. But now, I believe every woman should assert herself, say what she wants to say, and do what she wants to do. At the end of the day, I know I can protect myself. And so can you.

As you listen to your intuition, you will be able to create a deeper sense of safety and security for yourself. This inner voice becomes a guiding force, leading you away from situations that don't serve you and toward opportunities that enrich your life. It helps you set boundaries and stand up for yourself, fostering a life aligned with your true desires and values.

Moreover, tuning into your intuition opens the door to a wellspring of creativity and inspiration. You begin to receive new ideas and insights, enabling you to live a more impactful life. This intuitive wisdom can guide you in making decisions that resonate with your authentic self, helping you navigate complex situations with grace and confidence. By trusting your inner knowing, you empower yourself to step into a life of purpose and fulfillment, where you not only survive but thrive.

CHAPTER 18

TRUST

Trust yourself to live with courage. I know you might feel fear. I know it might seem impossible to do what you know needs to be done, but trust will support you.

Don't try to figure out your finances or home all at once. Avoid getting distracted by the bigger picture. Instead, focus on the present moment and lean into trust. By doing so, you'll feel more love, empowerment, and readiness to move forward with trust as your foundation.

Unconditional trust helps you have courage, be brave, take action, and receive all the inspiration that is yours. You have everything you need, right here, right now, inside of you.

I can tell you this because I have come to rely on my ability to trust myself. I've discovered that trusting myself has actually been a gift of mine. I found that because it was hard for me to trust other people, my ability to trust myself became stronger. I've done a lot of things that I had no proof that I could actually do, but I trusted myself so much that

I did it. The self-trust became even stronger once I decided to unshackle myself.

After my divorce, I didn't know how I was going to afford to keep the house or pay my bills while raising four little children, but I rode the horse of trust. I dug my heels in deep and witnessed the power of self-trust.

Self-trust only arises in the moments of deep fear and doubt. This will be the place you find yourself wanting to break. When you step out on your own, you will start to lose trust. But this is where you need to strengthen your self-trust. Deepen it. You know that you can do this. You are one of the strongest women you know.

I know because of what you have been through.

Trusting yourself is challenging, especially if you've experienced abuse or mistreatment. Trust is often the first thing that gets damaged in such situations. It's ironic that when your ability to trust has been shattered, the only way to heal and move forward is to rebuild that trust *in yourself*. Despite the difficulty, you must learn to trust yourself again.

We often struggle to trust others, which can also make us doubt our own abilities. However, trusting yourself is essential. Have confidence in your decisions. Tell yourself, "I'm going to do this. I'm going to _____," and trust that you can achieve it. **Embrace your inner strength and believe in your capacity to succeed.**

Start with trusting what you already know. Trust the gut feelings that have been grabbing your attention. I know this is hard to do, but remember, trust is like a house you build brick-by-brick. It's not a single pillar or block but a compilation of small moments that add up to trust. So begin small.

Start small with trusting your intuition.

When trust is broken—in a marriage, friendship, business partnership, or religion—it can feel like your entire house has been bulldozed, and all the trust you've built is gone. As if every "trust" brick is flattened. When I faced betrayal in a former relationship, whether from a lie or an addiction, I felt like my whole house had been destroyed. When the most catastrophic part of my relationship ended, I stood back and assumed the entire house was gone. But when I stepped closer and examined, I realized there were still some bricks left. The foundation was still there and symbolized the self trust I still had. Though my house of trust I had built with my partner was destroyed, my own self trust still remained as the foundation.

Building self-trust involves recognizing that even after devastation, you can start rebuilding brick-by-brick. Each small moment of trust you create for yourself adds up, and over time, you'll see a new, stronger foundation emerge. Over time, you will rebuild your house.

I know that this is not an easy path.

This experience has tested me to my core. But in the moments that pushed me to the breaking point, I would begin to see that I actually had proof of self-trust. I had proof from all the times I had trusted myself in the past. And those memories reminded me that I could do it again in the future.

I once felt a lot of guilt and shame for not seeing when betrayal was coming, but I have learned to love myself for those times. I have been able to look back and notice that my intuition had actually warned me. Despite doubting myself, my intuition would always persist. Even when I didn't listen, my intuition would not leave me.

It felt as if God seemed to be guiding me every step of the way, urging me to look down at my feet. It was there that I saw the outline of the home I had once built. It may have had broken windows and missing doors, but it was built on a foundation of trust that still remained. In that moment, I felt encouraged to focus on the instances when I'd trusted myself and succeeded. Instead of getting frustrated with myself for not listening to my intuition, I would make note of all the places I HAD listened. Intuition is our greatest guide. We have been given this internal compass and all we need to do is listen to it.

I really began to notice my relationship with trust when I began to run businesses. This was one place where I always trusted myself. This is where I began to strengthen my trust muscle. And because it began to grow strong in the realm of business, I was able to start using trust outside of business as well.

Trusting yourself is one of the deepest ways to strengthen your intuition—your strongest ally. Intuition is like a relationship. The more you listen to and trust it, the more likely you will be to rely on it in the future. If you often ignore your intuition—when it urges you to stay home, call a friend, or bring a meal—you won't build a strong relationship with it. Then, when your intuition warns you about something significant, like avoiding a dangerous situation or making a life-changing decision, you might not listen to it because you haven't developed trust in it.

I encourage you to reflect on moments in your life when you trusted yourself. Note them. Acknowledge them. As you begin to see where you HAVE listened to your intuition, you will begin to build this deep self-trust.

I run retreats for women from all over the world. At these retreats I lead the women in a special ceremony. In this ceremony, participants are invited to write down their negative beliefs about themselves. Every negative thought they think about themselves, they write it down. Any negative belief someone else believes about them, they write it down. Everything they no longer want to believe about themselves, they write it down.

Then they rip the page out. One at a time, I have these women re-read their negative and harmful thoughts they have about themselves. Once they are done reading them one last time, they light the paper on fire. I instruct them to hold onto these beliefs (this paper) until they physically can no longer or they will be burned. I emphasize clinging to them tightly until they have no other choice but to release them, and watch them burn.

After they clear out their negative beliefs, I help them build trust through new words and new thoughts. But instead of the regular affirmations, I advocate for these women to write *confirmations*.

Once they have watched their paper burn to ashes, I invite them to fill up the space they now have in their hearts and minds with confirmations that those beliefs were not true.

For example, if they wrote down "I am not a good friend" after they watched it burn, they would write down a confirmation of when they were a good friend.

If they initially wrote down "I am a bad wife," then to confirm this is not true, they write a time they can recall being a good wife.

Confirmations are more powerful than affirmations because they acknowledge instances where they've proven their worth to themselves.

Many women I have worked with have faced deep deception. They were told things by a loved one, partner, or friend that they wanted to believe, but the actions never matched the words. This begins to build a lack of trust with their intuition because they so badly wanted to believe that the words they were hearing were true. This lack of self-trust leads women to be flooded with negative thoughts and doubt.

I want to emphasize the importance of ignoring the negative voices and seeking confirmation of self-trust. Affirmations can feel insincere and are rarely strong enough to change the patterns and thoughts that get lodged within our minds. I have found that confirmations are tangible evidence of self-love and trust. Confirmations change the state we are in, allowing us to create new patterns. Confirmations are PROOF to YOU that you **do** listen to your intuition. As you begin to document instances when you **do** listen to your intuition, you will begin to trust yourself more. As you notice new actions that are being inspired by your intuitions, it is like depositing bricks to rebuild your self-trust.

If you would like to do this exercise with me right now, watch the video HERE and download the Confirmation Worksheet by clicking the QR CODE.

Our ability to cultivate our intuition can also be challenged and broken within orthodox religions and communities. From a young age, I was taught to outsource my intuition. Growing up in a high-demand religious faith brought many blessings and values that I still cherish, but it also had consequences. I was taught to give my God-given intuition and discernment to others, and I was told I wouldn't even receive this gift until I was eight years old. In this religion, I was taught that intuition and the promptings of the Holy Ghost were the same thing, and that we didn't receive this until we were eight years old.

I never doubted this religion until it was time for my daughter to get baptized. I had committed my life to this religion and was a good-standing member. I had never been challenged in my faith. However, a few months before her baptism, I had a thought: *What if she already has the gift of the Holy Ghost?* This question caught me off guard. It wasn't a lightning strike of revelation, but it was a small, persistent thought that was always lingering in my mind.

As her baptism approached, I noticed my daughter exhibiting intuition and "Holy Ghost" moments, which contradicted my religious teachings that she wouldn't have this gift until she was baptized. This realization put me at a significant crossroads, as it was the first principle of the church that I found myself questioning.

While I was deconstructing the layers of religion, I started learning that my spirituality had been stripped from me when I was a young girl. Religion had been packaged up in this beautiful box with a tag that said, "Spirituality is inside this box." When I opened it up, I realized I didn't have spirituality; I only had religion. And those are two very different things. I was never taught how to talk to God myself. I had to outsource my intuition to a set of commandments and rules. Instead of allowing my intuition to lead me to communicate with God, I ignored my intuition and did what I was told.

If I had a sin and felt I needed to repent, I couldn't call upon God and take care of it myself. I had to talk to the local bishop, who happened to be a forty-five-year-old accountant with no spiritual dominion over what God wanted for me. From a young age, I was taught to submit my godly plan to another person, specifically a male. This was reinforced when I got married young and was told I had to submit to my husband for blessings for myself and my children. If someone was sick, I didn't have the power and authority to call on God for a miracle; only my husband did.

I learned I could not send my children to school with a blessing for the beginning of the school year; only my husband could. Why? Because I was a woman. I started not being okay with that and I began learning through intuition and my experience of God directly talking to me.

I DIDN'T NEED SOMEONE ELSE TO DO IT FOR ME.

I realized that I don't need to submit to a man to talk to God. In fact, God speaks directly to me. Growing up, I was always taught to ask if the church was true. In the church's culture, I was instructed to seek confirmation that I was on the right path by asking if the church was true. I did this numerous times, and while I never experienced an overwhelming lightning strike of affirmation, I did feel a sense of peace that, in those moments, the church was something good for me.

As I reflected on my spiritual limitations, a thought occurred to me: *Why don't you ask if this is **not** true?* No one had ever given me permission to do that. I noticed that this conversation was always controlled by fear, and the only idea we were ever given was to ask if it is *true*. Then, one day, God spoke to me: "Why don't you ask me if this is not true?" At first, I thought, *I'm not allowed to do that.*

With the most honest, open, and terrified heart—because I wasn't sure I wanted to know the answer—I knelt down and asked, "God, is this religion I'm a part of true?" That's when I received my lightning bolt. It was a confirmation bigger than any message God had ever sent to me.

The heavens opened. I saw it, felt it viscerally, and heard, "This church is not true." Then came the words, "I am so proud of you for finally asking the *right* question. It's you and me now."

God was waiting for me to take back my own authority and spiritual connection to Him. But to disregard, throw away, step back from everything I had been building inside religion my entire life? He told me, "This is not your way. You and I communicate directly. I will teach you the way of God. I will show you miracles. I will help you perform miracles. You do not have to continue to be a Mormon to find me. In fact, now that you have sifted through all the distractions, you have cleared this vessel to come straight to me. I can talk to you directly now. I don't have to go through your young women's teachers to give you a message. I don't have to go through your spouse, bishop, or prophet. I will go straight to you."

And that is the moment power filled my body, and my life took a completely different direction. That was the moment I witnessed myself looking down at my hands, realizing I held a match, and then intentionally igniting my own home (metaphorically) on fire.

But what did that mean for me if I actually was willing to light my house on fire? That meant there were parts of me I had to watch burn, and there were relationships I would need to torch. That's when I realized this could impact all of the areas of my life. I knew I would lose many, many friends because of this. I would lose respect in my community. I would lose trust with my neighbors. I knew I would lose everything that I thought was important.

God said, "Trust in me. You will rebuild the correct way. You will rebuild a house and a foundation that withstands the challenges that will come your way." I watched my entire life start to burn from the edges of my feet as the fire moved forward slowly.

Now, here's the thing. When you choose to light your own house on fire, you know when a fire is about to start. I got to step back and move out of the way of its fury and the potential of burning me alive. Did I feel the fire, its fury, its flames, and its heat? Yes, because I was standing next to it.

BUT IT DID NOT ENGULF ME.

When you willingly choose to let go of certain parts of your life, you retain control over the process. You decide where the fire burns, and as a result, you cannot be consumed by it. This act of surrendering leads to gaining trust in yourself. I remember vividly the moment when I surrendered to God's plan for me and trusted in myself. Although this new path was unfamiliar and daunting, it became another building block in constructing my foundation of self-trust. It was here that I truly learned to trust myself.

CHAPTER 19

CHALLENGING BELIEFS

I was raised with beliefs that felt like the utmost truth. I was loyal to keeping those beliefs close to me, never straying. But here, I will talk about how leaving organized religion and finding God in "untraditional" ways has led my beliefs to change. I now teach my children about topics like alcohol and sex, and how those things physically, mentally, and emotionally affect them, instead of how they affect their worthiness and divine "plan."

"You've changed," my friend said to me. She didn't mean it in a nice way. She was telling me this because my growth meant I had changed and that was uncomfortable for *her*.

If I were to sit down for lunch today with my twenty-five-year-old self, we wouldn't see eye to eye on everything. The majority of my beliefs, habits, and patterns of thinking wouldn't align with hers. If I could go back in time and talk to her, I would emphasize the importance of humility in the constantly challenging and re-examining of one's beliefs and narratives. No belief or story is final; everything I think and believe now will change, and that's okay. Embrace it, lean into it. I view the comment "you've changed" as one of the highest forms of flattery because change equals growth. I'm really proud of how far I've come.

When the time comes that ignorance ceases to benefit you, you'll inevitably seek knowledge. In my pursuit of self-liberation, I began to scrutinize deeply entrenched beliefs. The concept of a savior—an external divine entity—underwent intense examination within me. My beliefs changed from the Savior *saving* me to him being a friend, a constant, a holy prophet and healer. I once relied on the Savior coming back to save me, but as I dove deeper into my spirituality, I decided that my saving is my responsibility. I rely on the Savior's words and actions to help me live a life of service, kindness, boldness, and hope.

While I am no longer affiliated with the LDS (Mormon) Church, I still abstain from drinking alcohol. However, my decision is no longer rooted in fear of worthiness or moral judgment. Instead, I choose not to drink because I believe it's not conducive to my health. I prioritize avoiding impairment and potential harm to myself and others. Avoiding alcohol helps me maintain clarity and better connection with myself, others, and God.

Similarly, my approach to tithing reflects my departure from organized religion while maintaining certain core values. Though I have chosen to leave organized religion, I still keep many values I was taught as very sacred to me. For example, the law of tithing to me is a principle to show to God you can sacrifice your monetary gatherings and give back. I don't think it matters who you give them to; what matters is the willingness to take what you have earned and give to someone else. Though I no longer adhere to traditional practices, such as giving to the church, I still hold the principle of sacrifice dear. For me, tithing is about demonstrating gratitude by sharing a portion of my earnings with causes I believe in, such as local shelters or nonprofits. I've embraced the essence of tithing and personalized it to align with my own spiritual journey. I'm grateful for my upbringing in the Mormon church, as it provided me with a foundation of values that I've chosen to integrate into my spiritual journey in my own unique way.

As I prepare to discuss sensitive topics like the law of chastity with my children, I've shifted away from associating these laws solely with rules to now governing with a value system and not with judgment. For instance, my approach to teaching my daughter about sex has evolved. Instead of conveying outdated notions like premarital sex makes one unworthy or disappointing to God, I emphasize the sacredness of the body. I explain to her that engaging in sex is an intimate exchange of energy, where one shares their soul with another and accepts the other's in return. I encourage her to be discerning about whom she shares this bond with, stressing the importance of understanding the energetic connection before committing to marriage. I encourage her to be very wise about when and with whom she decides to share that connection. While I advocate for responsible and meaningful sexual relationships, I discourage reckless or casual encounters. I believe that sexual intimacy is a deeply spiritual act akin to embodying the Divine, and it's crucial for her to comprehend this before making lifelong commitments to another person. It is very important that you see how your spirits interchange with one another because sexual intercourse is one of the most sacred things you can do with your partner. It is acting as if you are a god and a goddess when you interchange energies. I would never tell my daughter to go and marry and commit her life to someone else without knowing how they energetically meet each other.

Don't you dare get married to have sex, like I did. It's a tragedy to rush into marriage solely for the sake of fulfilling sexual desires, as I once did in my own hasty three-month engagement driven by lust. I will encourage my children, no matter how many people it offends, to have sex with the person they are committing their soul to, in a respectable time frame and in an emotionally mature environment. I also teach my children that the danger of having sex with someone you don't love can trick you into *thinking* you might love somebody. I make it a priority to teach my children, regardless of any potential backlash, the importance of engaging in sexual intimacy within the context of a *committed* relationship and in a mature emotional environment.

Additionally, I educate them about the pitfalls of engaging in sexual activity with someone they don't genuinely love, as it can lead to confusion between lust and genuine affection. In my own experience, I found myself convinced I was in love simply because I had only been intimate with one person—my former spouse—whom I had sex with for the first time on our honeymoon night. Unfortunately, this lack of experience led me to mistake physical attraction for love, prolonging a relationship that should have ended sooner.

It became apparent that without a clear understanding of what true love and meaningful sexual connection entailed, I had accepted the lack of tenderness, foreplay, and emotional connection as genuine intimacy because I didn't know any different.

Challenging Beliefs

When we aren't taught, we accept whatever is given.

Without prior experience or proper guidance, we often default to accepting the first and only example as the definitive way.

This realization highlights the importance of entering into sexual relationships with someone we genuinely love and understand lest we sacrifice authentic love for fleeting experiences mistaken as such.

We don't realize the impact we have on teenagers with our examples, our words, and most importantly the way we make them feel.

Within certain church circles, controversial topics like *sex* are often approached with analogies such as the "chewed gum lesson." In this lesson, a teacher passes around a piece of chewed gum and equates having sex with being considered "chewed gum." The underlying message is clear: engaging in premarital sex diminishes your worth. You are like a piece of gum that has been used, deeming you less valuable to a man of God. I vividly recall being subjected to this lesson as a thirteen-year-old girl.

While some individuals, both within and outside the faith, may claim to have never encountered such teachings, I am living proof that this lesson was indeed taught because I was also the one who taught it. With great shame, I admit that less than six years ago, while serving as a leader to young women in the church, I had the audacity to impart this message onto a group of impressionable fourteen-year-old girls. The responsibility for this reprehensible act rests solely with me, and I recognize that I will be held accountable for it. Even now, I am filled with regret and I feel compelled to personally apologize to each of those girls, many of whom are now in college or on service missions. I cannot believe I propagated such harmful teachings, but I was merely perpetuating what I had been taught myself. This highlights the significant impact of beliefs being passed down from women to girls.

The stigma surrounding premarital sex within religious contexts often overshadows discussions about the dynamics of sex within marriage, especially in cases where one partner mistreats the other. Consent, respect, and kindness are neglected topics in these discussions.

The true lesson should revolve around choosing partners who treat you with kindness, respect, and love, irrespective of marital status. This is the standard I am instilling in my children—not dictating *when* to have sex, but emphasizing the importance of selecting partners who value and honor them. It's not about adhering to a predetermined timeline; it's about choosing partners who genuinely respect and cherish you.

There's a prevailing belief that leaving the church equates to being cut off from God, but I aim to challenge that narrative. Whether you're questioning your faith, standing firm in it, or have no religious faith at all, I want to boldly declare that you can encounter God within or beyond the confines of organized religion. To those who've judged me for leaving the church—how dare you! I've never felt closer to God. My conversations with Him have never been more frequent, and His purpose for me has never been clearer. In my thirty years of devout worship, I never felt a deeper understanding of God than I do now. **We must reshape the narrative, casting less judgment and**

acknowledging that no single church holds absolute truth. Truth resides solely between you and God.

Understanding my history with religion is crucial. I was unwaveringly committed to the church, dedicating my life, heart, assets, time, and service to it. I held esteemed leadership roles, fulfilling callings typically "reserved" for older women, while raising my children. Stepping away was the most significant moment in my life up to that point. I was fervently devoted, not wavering or lukewarm in my beliefs. I defended doctrine and even taught it as a Gospel Doctrine instructor before I turned thirty—an intimidating task within the church hierarchy. Stepping away from the church was a monumental decision for me, marking a significant moment in my personal history. My unwavering dedication was evident; I engaged in spirited doctrinal debates, held intimidating teaching positions, and invested deeply in my faith. My departure signifies a profound trust in God beyond what the church ever demanded. It's a testament to my unwavering commitment and a profound leap of faith.

I was fully invested. All in. To step away signifies an unparalleled trust in God's guidance throughout my spiritual journey.

In my journey of spiritual growth, I've come to realize that I don't have to wait for a divine calling. God has already called me, and I am taking full responsibility for answering that call personally, in direct connection with God. Remaining within the church doesn't necessarily mean fulfilling my spiritual duties. There's a misconception that attending church absolves one of their responsibility to nurture their faith at home. Unlike those who rely solely on Sunday School for their children's spiritual education, I've recognized the need to take charge of teaching my kids about God, especially since we no longer attend church. They won't learn about figures like Moses or Esther unless I actively teach them. God has impressed upon me the importance of taking radical accountability for my children's spiritual upbringing outside of organized religious structures. It's up to me to determine what truths resonate within our family, guided by my personal relationship with God. **They don't go to a church "school" where anyone's opinions and life experiences get to be intertwined with actual truth. I get to decide what truth remains in our family, and that's between me and God only.**

CHAPTER 20

REVISED NARRATIVE

A profound lesson I learned while walking the path of divorce was how easily a narrative could be birthed and then altered. An event could happen, but the narrator telling the story has the ability to retell the story in his own "tone." This is how it went for me and my former partner. The same story could have completely different narratives.

I witnessed this years ago when I was sitting in my church's front foyer. I was minding my own business when I overheard a neighbor telling another neighbor about his family trip to Disneyland. I was curious about this subject, so I listened in, uninvited. He was telling them how amazing the food was. He spent time going into detail describing all the delicacies he found—how amazing the churros were, how many macaroons he ate. As I listened to him speak, it was clear to me that his experience at Disneyland was heavily influenced by the food. That is all he was talking about, and he didn't mention a single other part other than what they ate.

Rising: Fearless Women Rebelling

I found it interesting that, not five minutes later, another neighbor came in and asked about their family trip, and the man didn't share the same story. This time, he was telling the person all about the rides and which ones they went on. He told them all about the wait times and how the crowds were. He described how they used their fast passes and talked about some tricks he had to eliminate standing in the lines. He didn't mention food one single time. My mind was actually blown when I heard him talking and I was a little confused as to why these stories didn't match up at all. I remember thinking, *man, these stories don't even sound like the same trip*.

Not even a few more minutes went by when again, he began talking to another person. I was extra curious this time and made it much more clear I was eavesdropping as I scooted closer to him. I wanted to see if we would get a different Disney story. And to my surprise, again, with this third neighbor, he shared a completely different account about his Disney trip. His message and focus was on the time he spent with his family and how it meant so much to be with his children. He spoke about how his son would graduate soon and how this family trip was the highlight of this year. He did not hit on the food or the rides they experienced. It was solely focused on how his family bonded together. I was so intrigued with how all three of his stories seemed like completely different experiences, yet it was all the same Disneyland trip.

He had indeed eaten the churro, waited in the long lines, and enjoyed the time with his children, but the differing narrative of the accounts was based on how he chose to narrate it. Was he sharing about the same vacation in very different ways depending on who the listener was? All

Revised Narrative

three accounts seemed like different trips because he chose to FOCUS on different things as he shared. Maybe the differences were based on how the listeners would accept the story. Or maybe the story changed because he simply chose different audiences. It was a "read the room" situation in which, depending on who asked, the accounts were different.

This taught me a profound lesson that we will retell our life's stories with whatever narrative we want. We will find what we focus on. This also can feel dangerous when other people recount *your* life stories and find parts of it to focus on that makes it feel like it was a completely different story.

I remember the pain I felt when people would gossip about parts of my divorce and choose parts to focus on that made it sound like a different couple's divorce. Many times it felt unjust and untrue how other people narrated *my* stories according to *their* audience and focus. "Robyn got divorced because she had an emotional affair," one said. "Robyn finally got divorced. That girl stayed for way too long and always deserved better. She endured so much shit in her marriage," said another. The reality of me getting divorced is not in question, but the narrator and how they chose to share about my divorce is where differing accounts happened.

Did I leave my marriage because I found emotional support from another person during the final months of my marriage and that person happened to be a man? Did I have an emotional affair? Those who choose to focus on THIS piece rob my former partner of the accountability he should accept for the years of neglect, abandonment, and mistreatment and diminish my resilience in the marriage and my bravery in leaving.

This focus puts blame on one single assumption and wipes away the years of betrayal, addiction, neglect, and mistreatment I endured. This focus makes me the villain and erases my courage for walking out.

Those who choose to focus on the mistreatment I endured from my former partner make him the villain in the story and steal away the years of service and dedication he gave to our family and free me and my toxic "holier-than-thou" mentality I proudly wore during our marriage.

The same stories will be told according to who is sharing them and the only one that you need to put energy into is where you focus in yours.

Some would say me leaving organized religion must have caused my divorce while others share that when I left, something changed in me and my light shone brighter than before. I've heard people say, "Ever since Robyn left the church, her life has spiraled out of control. I bet that was a huge reason why she got divorced." Then another person said, "Robyn left the church and stepped into her power because of it. That girl has never shone brighter."

Either way, the fact that I left organized religion is the same. The accounts differed because of the narrators and the audience and energy they were sharing it with. Their focus could be that they assumed it was the start of self-destruction or that it was the start of self-acceptance. Same story, different narrators.

Yet, the greater lesson I learned is you can't control how people narrate your stories, but you can control how YOU do. This comes with great responsibility because just like my neighbor who chose to focus on three separate things when retelling his experience, we get to choose our focus. We have the power to choose the parts of our lives we want to focus on. We choose how the narration is presented and who receives it. We choose if it's positive and powerful or if it's negative and laced with victimhood. Do not outsource your life's narration to other people, and certainly make sure you're reading your own story in a way that inspires positivity, power, and passion. You have the power to narrate your story and no matter how dark, painful, lonely, and hard you feel it is, you get to choose how you retell it. You have the power to live in the energy you choose as you experience life. I know there are places you can find where there is love, abundance, happiness, and joy in the same story you feel is consumed with pain and sorrow.

You find what you focus on. You are the narrator.

CHAPTER 21

THE DEATH OF THE PLEASER

When I moved into my new home in 2019, the first thing that I put into every child's room was a fire escape ladder. As a safety queen, I made sure each room on the second floor was equipped and prepared. Little did I know I would soon be facing a different kind of fire—a fire that would consume the carefully constructed façade of my life.

In my relentless pursuit of people-pleasing, I unwittingly struck the match that set my own house ablaze. I had become so adept at meeting the expectations of others that I lost sight of my true self. Each act of compliance felt like feeding fuel to a fire that was slowly devouring my authenticity.

The inferno of transformation began with a spark of realization—a moment of clarity amid the suffocating smoke of conformity. I had danced to the tune of others' expectations for too long, sacrificing my own dreams and desires on the altar of approval. As the flames of confrontation and honesty engulfed me, I realized that this fire was not to be feared but embraced.

Rage surged through me like wildfire, tearing through the landscape of my existence and leaving nothing untouched. Relationships crumbled under the weight of newfound assertiveness, institutions of comfort shattered, and the familiar terrain of my reality was reshaped beyond recognition. Yet, amid the chaos and devastation, I found a profound sense of liberation.

In the crucible of destruction, I discovered the power of reclaiming agency over my life. Yes, I had willingly ignited the blaze that consumed the old, but in doing so, I forged a path to renewal and resilience. The flames became my allies, guiding me through the transformative process and illuminating the way to a more authentic existence.

As I mourned the loss of the familiar and grappled with uncertainty, I found solace in the knowledge that true growth often emerges from the ashes of despair. The journey through destruction was fraught with doubt and guilt, yet each day brought new opportunities for growth and self-discovery.

Emerging from the flames, I found myself reborn—a phoenix rising from the ashes of my former life. Fresh relationships blossomed, opportunities beckoned, and the scars of the past became reminders of my strength and endurance. The road ahead was not without challenges, but through the crucible of transformation, I gained the courage to embrace a future filled with possibility and purpose.

The death of the pleaser marked a profound turning point in my journey. Though the fires of change scorched the landscape of my existence, they also cleared the path for growth, renewal, and self-discovery. Standing amid the smoldering ruins of my past, I am filled with gratitude for the fire that forged me into the resilient and authentic person I am today.

CHAPTER 22

THE GRIEF OF THE LOST DREAM

We grieve the loss of the dream we had hoped for but never actually had. One of the most painful parts of my divorce is that many parts of my relationship were pretty "good." It wasn't neglect and abandonment *all* the time. It wasn't *always* disconnection, addictions, and stonewalling. In fact, it was filled with a lot of really great moments. We grew up together. We had babies together. We built our businesses together. We had a really beautiful life, which made it really confusing to me when there were parts that were painful at a level I could not comprehend.

Something that originally caught my attention when I met my former partner as a teen was his work ethic. He came from a family of hard workers, and they were championed in the community for how hard they were willing to work. They made a great living for themselves through their ability to work more than others. I remember my parents and friends pointing this out about him to note how lucky I was to have someone who could "work like that."

What I learned years into my relationship was that this work ethic was rooted deeply and was morphing into more of an addiction than I wanted to acknowledge. Though it was a noble quality, anything good can turn into a vice if you allow it to. Work became my partner's life, purpose, and passion. It felt as if his priority wasn't me, or even the kids that came later on. Work was his marriage and first priority. The first time I recall being betrayed was when I realized he was having an affair with work and I would have to accept it or leave.

This was a tender topic in our relationship from the start. What I'd thought was a badge of honor when I was a young girl turned into a real discrepancy for me as we grew into our marriage. I did not feel okay with waking up alone most mornings and eating dinner by myself most nights. I started to resent his work and felt jealous of his commitment to it over me. I understood we had to make a living and work hard but felt like the time he spent at work was absolutely overkill. I received no validation that this imbalance of work over family was wrong, and he and others constantly assured me that this was normal. His dad and brothers did the same—committing themselves to work more than to their wives. No matter how much discrepancy I felt about his complete lack of work-home balance, there was no solution or possible change. I was told this was just how it was and I should be grateful for his ability to work. This felt unfair. I had to be pinned as either the ungrateful wife who constantly nagged her partner to slow down the work or the cool wife who shut up and assumed this was how it was. There was never a world where anyone would recognize that he was absolutely addicted to work. Addiction was too harsh of a word, so it was convoluted into a quality of highest praise: what an incredibly *hard worker*.

The Grief of the Lost Dream

This was the standard in our marriage from day one. We only spent a handful of hours together each night, and when a person is working that much, they honestly don't want to connect with anyone. He was usually cold, quiet, snippy, and grumpy, so the hours I craved to be with him daily always felt like a disappointment when he got home. I knew immediately in my relationship that this was not what I thought love should be. I didn't feel loved. I didn't feel adored or wanted. I felt like I was a title—"wife"—and he gave no attention to me until work was done. And even then I got the scraps. For me, this was abuse. To be totally neglected and abandoned each day felt painful in ways I couldn't describe. To be over-the-moon giddy to see my husband when he walked through the doors at 9 p.m. only to be met with an underwhelming hello and little to no connection until we went to bed was rejection. This happened over and over, and looking back, I feel bad for the girl that kept waiting at the door thinking, *today is the day he will choose me*. It rarely happened.

I realized that this was just how it was going to be. No one else had any concern over this addiction, so he could simply continue to abuse his inability and unwillingness to provide connection and time for me. Not long into our marriage, I realized that starting my own business would save me from abandonment and rejection in the marriage. Before I knew it, we were both enthralled with our own work and becoming more like roommates day by day. As he was running his company and I was the primary caregiver for the children who came along while also running my business, we did the opposite of what time in a marriage does. We grew alone. We were ships passing in the night and our emotional and verbal connection was lacking. But our sex life—that felt better than average.

Most of our marriage was consumed with the hustle. We were in the depths of the grind, behavior we were modeling from watching our parents do the same. It was this known idea that in the early and precious years of marriage, we should completely disconnect and focus on building our lives financially. That meant starting companies and overworking.

But we were not just overworking, like staying an hour or two later at the office. We were overworking like leaving for work at 5 a.m. and coming home between 7 and 10 p.m. This is just how it was. From the beginning, I knew my soul had started to settle into "this is normal" and got complacent with the standard of our marriage.

For the first ten years, those who knew us would have agreed we were a really "happy couple." We didn't fight in public, we held hands, and we would kiss in front of people. I always used my over-the-top personality to be loud and flirty with him. I really tried to pour lightness and fun into my marriage as much as possible. Though we both overworked, we were pretty good at having a consistent date night routine.

From the outside looking in, we appeared to be a pretty badass power couple. We each owned our own businesses and each business was lucrative. We built our dream home before we both turned thirty. We had a lot of good couple friends we hung out with frequently. We traveled. We owned all the snowmobiles, trailers, RZRs, and fun things.

The Grief of the Lost Dream

We got along okay, but I always felt like I had to water myself down to be a version that could communicate with him. I'm a big talker, the kind who wants to catch up at the end of a day, pour dreams out of my mouth, talk about how our hearts feel. I'm a big dreamer. But this version of me could not live around my partner. It was not welcomed or appreciated. It was a part of me I had to be okay with not embodying because this relationship could only hold basic.

Basic conversation. Basic connection. Basic sex. Basic love. Honestly, I knew that to keep my marriage "thriving" at this basic level I had to get used to basic. So I did! I accepted the basic and as per usual, lived complacently. I worked to make my basic marriage the happiest it could be. But there are limits to basic. It could never hold the version of me that was big, and powerful, and deep. I could rarely talk and discuss parts of me that screamed to be heard. This is the part that held the most pain. I lived *parts* of my dream. So why did I have to leave?

I often found myself clinging tightly to any moment that just felt "normal," and still, to this day, I'm not even sure if the moments that I felt were "happy" were actual happiness. It's so painful for me to think about the lost dream of my family because I *had* the dream, for moments. It wasn't something we *never* accomplished. I lived it, I was in it. But then to see it threatened so many times from very simple ways all the way up to very traumatic ways still holds the most pain in me. I'm sure you have similar thoughts: *How could I ever leave? It's not that bad. Yes, I have moments that I know I shouldn't allow, but, look, for the most part, it's really beautiful.* Or maybe yours is more black and white. Maybe it's filled with more darkness than light, yet you still find yourself clinging to the dream. I honestly get it. One of the most confusing and painful parts of my divorce is that I had an okay marriage—for the most part. I loved my husband, and all I wanted in return was for him to love me back. There were moments, times and parts of it when things were going exceptionally well, and we were very high, and that's what made the moments that felt so hurtful sting even more.

What felt very tricky for me, and I'm sure you've experienced the same, is I was told that marriages are just hard. I got advice from many therapists, close family members, and confidants, and I never got a hard set "you should leave your husband" at the beginning. I watched my friends, siblings, and other family members have similar challenges in their marriages, so it felt like, *oh, this is just what it is.* I started to wear "marriage is hard" as a badge of honor. My marriage was hard, and I knew that we were very disconnected. I felt abandoned. We had a lot of confrontation and conflict in our marriage, but it was always laced with incredibly beautiful moments. It wasn't until years later—being in a relationship with a completely different foundation—that I realized maybe those moments in my first marriage weren't actually as beautiful or grand as I had made them. Maybe they were just mediocre happy moments, but I had aggrandized them to be more than they really were to make up for the abuse.

TRANSMUTE GRIEF WITH GRATITUDE FOR COMPLETE FREEDOM.

One of the most surprising things I experienced during my divorce process was meeting grief. Up until that time, I didn't know that I'd ever known grief. I've never had anyone super close to me pass away. I truly don't know that I had ever experienced grief. I remember being months

The Grief of the Lost Dream

into the divorce process and having moments of absolute clarity, peace, ease, and confidence. Then, without warning, like a wave crashing over me, I would be crippled with anxiety, fear, and depression. I went back to my therapist and said, "I don't understand. I'm doing so well. Everything feels so right, and then without any warning, I will be hit with this deep, deep, deep feeling." She looked up at me and said, "You have met grief." I was a little surprised because I always thought grief just came when someone passed away. She said, "Grief is part of this process, and it will come unexpectedly. Do not doubt yourself when grief hits, for it will pass." In that moment, I visualized grief as a wave. A wave is very symbolic for me. It symbolizes the ebbs and flows of the emotions anyone can feel. I soon put a gold chain around my neck with a pendant of a wave on it, and to this day I have not taken it off.

There was also a line in a Pearl Jam song that struck me in the deepest parts of grief: "I'll ride the wave where it takes me."[1] I knew I had to trust myself and trust the process and know that I would be led to the right place. I would be guided to take the next step, and I would know if I should turn right or left. The wave is very symbolic to me—and maybe it makes sense to you—because just like the ocean, life can be very calm, relaxing, and soothing, and without any warning can unleash a fury (grief) that can destroy anything in its path, but then always eventually settles. Grief, for me, is the number one emotion I felt most during my divorce. It was a feeling that took me to the bottom of my sorrow. Grief felt like the big daddy puff of all emotions. It's a little bit of anger, a little

---

[1] "Release," written by Eddie Vedder, Mike McCready, Stone Gossard, Jeff Ament, and Dave Krusen, recorded by Pearl Jam, Produced by Rick Parashar and Pearl Jam on *Ten,* track 11, August 27, 1991.

bit of anxiety—like panic hysteria. Grief is the most potent and profound emotion that I feel.

Here is my antidote for how to move through grief. The first thing you have to do is be able to accept it. You have to know what you're grieving and the pain that's accompanying it. Once you have taken the first step, you will have to transmute the grief and pain with gratitude. You can use a practice such as writing down every thought and emotion that comes with your grief. Or you could think it in your head. But when you're ready, you speak out everything you are grateful for with that specific situation or person.

For example, I was feeling grief about my marriage ending, so I accepted it, acknowledged the pain I felt and how disappointing it is that I had to get divorced. I sat with it and then asked myself, "What am I grateful for in my former marriage?" Resistance came. I let it pass through me, and I was able to speak out many words that I hadn't even been focusing on that I truly am grateful for because of my marriage. This truly took the grief and transmuted it into moments and memories of gratitude that I can now focus on and breathe into myself.

I want you to take a moment and write down anything you are grieving. I have left space below for you to write in. Write down specific details, and when you are done, you will then speak out what you are grateful for because of it. I am proud of you that you are willing to sit with grief. I know the feeling that is weighing down your chest and scratching up your lungs. I believe you have the capacity to move through grief and find gratitude. I am right here with you because I, too, have been where you are. Grief comes like a tidal wave out of nowhere and crashes us to the ground, but remember, like a wave, though it can be destructive, overwhelming, and powerful, it always calms and is one of the most beautiful things to witness.

RISE IN YOUR POWER

1. Pick a situation that you feel grief around.

2. Write out all of the grief you feel.

3. Acknowledge the emotions and then feel them.

4. Now write out everything that you are grateful for in that situation or relationship.

_____
_____
_____
_____
_____
_____
_____
_____
_____
_____
_____
_____
_____
_____

Rising: *Fearless Women Rebelling*

The Grief of the Lost Dream

The end of one dream does not mean the end of all dreams. It is in the space of loss that we have the ability to create new. We have the agency to design a dream that reflects our deepest desires and values. We need to honor the dreams we have lost while empowering ourselves to build new ones—dreams that are vibrant, authentic, and purely our own. Remember, the path of self-love is the foundation on which your new dreams will flourish. You have the potential to transform your grief into the fertile soil of possibility where the seeds of your TRUE potential can take root and grow. Don't mourn the vision of a future that will never come to pass. Instead, focus on the momentum you now have to create the dreams you have always wanted. In the wake of lost dreams, there is always a wave.

Ride the wave where it takes you.

CHAPTER 23

FROM VICTIM TO VICTOR

What if I told you that being a victim is merely a choice? Throughout generations, women have been conditioned to adopt a victim mentality. It's like it's ingrained in our feminine DNA to be a damsel in distress awaiting rescue. From relying on others for financial stability to seeking protection from men and salvation from religious institutions, we've outsourced our own authority, perpetuating a cycle of victimhood in our lives.

In observing women from previous generations, I've noticed a prevalent sense of victimhood among those who have come before me. There's a pervasive belief that everyone is wronging them, leaving them feeling constantly offended and hurt, yet rarely do they take accountability for their circumstances.

Being a victim or a victor is simply a choice. To transition from victim to victor requires embracing accountability. It means reclaiming our power and ceasing to outsource it to external sources. Whether it's financial independence, physical safety, or spiritual fulfillment, we must recognize that we hold the key to our own liberation.

Consider my own experience with my sexual assault. While such trauma affects countless women each year, the difference in how much these events impact us lies in how we choose to respond. Will we succumb to victimhood, allowing it to dictate our lives and lead us down paths of self-destruction? Or will we rise as victors, empowered to shape our own destinies?

I want to make a point that you can be a victim of an event, another person's actions, or even misfortune, but your *victimhood* can end there, on that day. The mentality that you choose to move forward with can determine how long you remain a victim.

On February 27, 2008, I WAS a victim of a brutal sexual assault. The next day, February 28, marked a critical choice for me: Would I allow this event to define my entire existence? Would I remain trapped in a victim mentality? Or would I begin the journey toward reclaiming my strength and autonomy? It wasn't a switch that was flipped and the change was done. It was a daily commitment to reclaiming my agency and refusing to let the trauma dictate my future.

No one would have blamed me if I'd remained the victim. They would have understood if I became depressed, quit school, and isolated myself. They would have also understood if this terrible experience spiraled me into drugs, alcohol, and more self-inflicted habits. I was allowed to be the victim after such a horrendous event, but I simply chose not to be.

I chose right then and there to be a victor. I chose to live as if I'd won the fight. I chose to live as if I was already healing. I chose to live as if it was something I had already moved through. I hadn't fully, but that mentality helped me move through it more quickly. And that's why within a year of my sexual assault, I was already teaching and empowering other women.

Twelve years later, as I was walking through my divorce, I already knew what I would choose: victor. I had already learned this was simply a choice. I chose to walk the lonely and terrifying path of divorce, but early on in the process, I chose a victor's mindset.

Was I abused in my former relationship? Yes. Was I wronged? Yes. Was there betrayal? Yes. And I let that land, I felt it for some time, and then I moved forward as the victor.

I took my divorce and alchemized it into something that molded me to be stronger and greater instead of weaker. A victim can't take care of themselves because they are imprisoned. But victory has a mentality of "this didn't happen *to* me, it happened *for* me. I can feed myself, I can nourish myself, and then I can help others." A victim can only worry about themselves; a victor worries about themselves first and then helps save other people.

Anyone going through a divorce, recovering from sexual assault, or leaving organized religion has every right to be a victim, but that prolongs their pain and keeps them in a selfish perspective where they cannot help and serve other people. A victim cannot help anyone else;

they're trying to stay alive. A victor can help other people through the same things they have experienced.

A lot of people have asked me, "What was the best way you found to heal from your sexual assault?" Obviously, therapy was amazing. Forgiveness was crucial. But the biggest, most important, most impactful way I moved through my sexual assault quickly and effectively was I went and served other people.

I used my experience and I healed other people through it. I could have remained a victim, and I might have never done this work. I might have never helped another woman. I would have been all about myself, stuck in my pain, *can't believe this happened to me*. But I chose freedom. A victim is selfish and can only help themselves; a victor changes lives and changes the world.

Heal yourself while healing others. It's simply a choice. I didn't get to do that because I'm special; I just knew that principle and decided to make a choice. I have applied the same principle with my divorce; I knew that through my divorce, I could help other women. But if you can't help yourself, you can't help anyone else. If you're starving, you are unable to serve anyone else because you are focused on staying alive. So much more joy in healing yourself comes when you are also healing other people.

Don't become an embodied victim. There's a distinction between experiencing victimization and embodying victimhood. While we may be victims in specific moments, we can't allow those moments to define us indefinitely. Each day presents an opportunity to choose our mentality, to decide whether we will remain ensnared in the past or move forward with resilience and strength.

Victimhood permeates even the most mundane aspects of our lives, from social exclusion to marital conflicts to body image struggles. Yet, in each scenario, we retain the power to choose our response. Will we wallow in victimhood, or will we seize the opportunity to rise above?

My journey from victim to victor began with monumental choices—overcoming sexual assault, leaving an abusive marriage, departing from organized religion—but it continues in the daily decisions I make. Every interaction and every setback present opportunities to reaffirm my commitment to empowerment over victimhood. Every single day you'll be faced with the choice of being a victim or a victor.

How do you respond when someone makes a mean comment online?

How do you respond when there's something unfair happening in your family?

How do you respond when a friend talks rudely about you or doesn't invite you to something?

A lot of women will victimize *themselves* so that they don't get invited to something or their friends leave them out.

You could be a victim of your church.

Maybe you were offended by someone in the neighborhood.

Someone said something to you that wronged or hurt you.

You can feel betrayed by a spouse with something as simple as just being lied to or not being a first priority. People fall victim to that all the time.

We're even victims to whether or not we like the food on our plates. "Oh, I can't eat that."

Choosing victorhood over victimhood is not a one-time decision but a daily practice. It requires a willingness to confront our conditioning, take ownership of our lives, and embrace the power of choice. While the path has challenges, the rewards of empowerment and self-actualization are immeasurable. So, let us cast off the shackles of victimhood and step boldly into our roles as architects of our own destinies.

I challenge you to observe your life and find the places where you have fallen into the pattern of victimhood.

I urge you to rewrite the story. Decide today that you do not need saving. Instead, you have the capacity to save others. It starts with a simple mindset shift. If you embody victorhood, you can change not only your world but the world of those around you.

CHAPTER 24

THE LOVE THAT HOLDS YOU CAPTIVE

Know that you can love AND leave. You can love deeply, yet know that staying in that love confines you, holding you back from growth and fulfillment. This might mean loving a partner who, despite your affection, is not aligned with your future path. It could be loving a religion that once provided comfort and community but no longer resonates with your beliefs and values.

Similarly, you can dearly love a mother or a friend, yet recognize the need to establish boundaries or create distance for your own well-being. This isn't about abandoning love but rather about honoring yourself and your journey.

You have to live in the paradox of loving and leaving. Love is the captor that keeps you in prison. It is possible to love *and* leave.

Love can be a captor, keeping us bound to situations or relationships that no longer serve our highest good. It takes courage to acknowledge this and take steps toward what is right for our personal growth and happiness.

It's a process of honoring the love and gratitude for what once was while also acknowledging the necessity of moving forward on a different path. This paradox invites us to hold space for conflicting emotions—love and grief, hope and uncertainty—as we navigate the complexities of life transitions.

I know that you've sat outside of your house in your car in tears. I know that you've reached out to friends and told them the truth, and then you wanted to run away because they just found out what it was like. And the reason you won't do a damn thing about it is that you love. I know you've sat in your closet hysterically crying because you have to leave something you actually love.

I know how painful it is to watch your neighbors gather at someone's home and you did not get invited because you left the church those neighbors all attend. I know it brings pain that you don't receive Christmas gifts simply because your underwear doesn't match theirs. I know what it feels like to no longer be accepted simply because you chose to stand in your truth. It feels unfair, almost like you have to trade one for the other. *You want to live in your truth? Well, then you are going to lose love from certain people, communities, or places.* But I know that you have everything it takes to live through this. You can love *and* leave.

I know that your relationship or church or family dynamic isn't ideal, but I know you also think that there is nothing better, and your love keeps you captive to this life. And I want you to know I understand it if you perhaps love the people, person, or community that shackles you. Most people who have been through abuse love their abusers. I know you've been taught that love is rare, so it feels like leaving something you love means you likely will never find love again.

But I'm a witness that love is abundant and can be found everywhere. I am also a witness that love has levels, and when you open your cup and love yourself, you can love others bigger. In the relationship I am in now with my fiancé, I have found love in places inside of me I never knew possible. I had settled for love that was surface level, basic, entry level—love that I thought was the best it could get. I'm here to tell you, you can get love at levels you never knew existed. I have someone who adores me, caresses me, craves me, ravishes me, and is thirsty for me. It's a love I never even knew was possible.

But I remember being in your shoes, thinking I had to trade one for the other: if I give up this love for truth, I may never find love again. This is where we live below our potential in love; we settle for mediocre and then glorify the basic love and turn it into more. I remember so many times when I felt so fully abandoned and unheard that my partner giving me even just one minute of his time felt like love at the tenth degree. But it was a façade. I was the dog that was only fed scraps. I was so malnourished and neglected that one ounce of attention felt like a feast. Love held me captive in my marriage, so I prolonged my pain through the divorce process and went back again and again. The love I had for my former partner kept me captive, even when I had profound spiritual experiences that told me it was time for me to leave that marriage. The love I had for him kept me coming back, which honestly just made the entire situation more traumatic and drawn out.

I get that you love your church but feel like you may not align with everything anymore. I understand that you love your mom but may need to put some boundaries up. I get that your best time is with your friend, but now it's time to distance yourself. I understand loving a spouse while having exact clarity that you have to divorce them. I understand the pain and confusion you feel when you have conflicting feelings of loving someone or something deeply, while also knowing it is time to end the relationship or depart. We're told love can save and is the healer of all.

So how painful is it when the love you have for your spouse cannot get them to change their addictions? Or when you love your spouse but your spouse is abusing you? Maybe you love your religion, the practices, and the values it's brought into your life, but you know you no longer can stay. **Love, unfortunately, can keep us captive.**

Family dynamics can be incredibly challenging, and it's something we often hesitate to discuss openly. We may deeply love our family members while also experiencing difficult and sometimes hurtful relationships with them. There's an unspoken expectation that because they're family, we should accept without question their disrespect, abandonment, or control.

Have you ever been at lunch with someone who bluntly admits that their relationship with their mom isn't great? Probably not. Instead, you might hear someone mention how their mom constantly critiques their parenting decisions.

Should we just tolerate this behavior because it's family? How often have you heard a friend say, "My dad is amazing," but then she adds that he's meeting her ex-husband for lunch, which makes her uncomfortable? Are we obligated to endure these unhealthy dynamics simply because of familial ties?

I want to challenge this notion and say emphatically, "No, we don't have to accept this."

I hold deep affection for my mom, even though she isn't always present for me. I admire her, yet I struggle with her criticisms of my parenting. I value her, yet I long for the affirmation that she's proud of me. I cherish her efforts, but sometimes feel a sense of burden when seeking her support. I acknowledge that my family's love may come with conditions, yet I find solace in maintaining some level of connection rather than none at all. Loving someone can indeed be complex, often intertwined with conditions that shape our relationships.

I deeply care about my family, which is why I feel compelled to maintain my connection with them. However, the truth is, the superficiality of our relationship causes me significant emotional pain.

I know I'm not alone in grappling with these feelings, and I don't claim to have all the answers.

Are we bound by obligation to maintain relationships simply because of blood ties?

Should we continue in relationships that operate on conditions rather than on unconditional love?

Is it wise to endure family relationships that don't nurture our emotional well-being?

How often do we stay in difficult situations "for the sake of our children"? We sometimes believe we can shield our loved ones from pain by staying. How long do we remain in marriages to protect our children from disruption? How frequently do we stay within a religious community for the sake of our children? How often do we tolerate mistreatment from our parents so our kids can have grandparents in their lives? How many times do we maintain friendships solely for the benefit of our friends' children having playmates nearby?

We may believe we're shielding our children from pain by staying put, but in reality, we might be denying them opportunities to learn and grow through adversity. In the process, we sacrifice our own peace of mind, health, completeness, happiness, and capacity to love—all in an attempt to manage the pain of others.

One of my greatest fears when I contemplated leaving my marriage was whether I was being selfish, knowing it would disrupt my children's lives and burden them with pain. This concern kept me in my marriage far longer than I should have stayed. I was consumed with how this divorce would affect them and f*** them up. When I finally couldn't take it anymore and I would leave my marriage, thinking I was messing up my children was the one single thing that turned me around and made me walk back ten different times.

I've had to come to the awareness that while the divorce *has* caused pain for my children, the greater pain would have been for them to see their mom accept less. The greater pain would have been for them to see their mother stay in something that stifled her. When I get sad that my children come from a multi-home family, I have to remember that this pain from the divorce is not as big as the joy, freedom, and high standard that I've now set for my children. Yes, there's pain. Yes, they'll have trauma from this. Yes, they'll need therapy. Yes, they'll need healing. But I trust that the joy, power, and self-confidence they see in me will rub off more on them. I trust it will permeate more than the pain that was caused by my divorce.

I am teaching my children to maintain their individuality and autonomy in relationships, even with those they love deeply, such as family and friends. By fostering a strong sense of self-worth and encouraging open communication, I help them understand that their needs and boundaries are valid and deserving of respect. We regularly discuss the importance of mutual respect and equality, emphasizing that love should never require sacrificing their well-being or freedom. Through both example and open dialogue, I aim to empower them to recognize and navigate unhealthy dynamics, ensuring they never feel captive or compromised in their connections with others, no matter how close or cherished those relationships may be.

We love each other so deeply. And that love can hold us captive even in the most abusive situations.

CHAPTER 25

ANXIETY'S ALLY

In a world that often values strength over vulnerability, many of us have become experts in the art of numbing our emotions. We've been conditioned to believe that showing our feelings is a sign of weakness, that being vulnerable is the same as being powerless. So, we lock away our fears, bury our sadness, and ignore our anxieties, hoping that by doing so we can shield ourselves from pain.

What if I told you that by numbing our emotions we're not protecting ourselves but rather setting the stage for anxiety to take root and flourish? What if the key to finding true strength and resilience lies not in suppressing our feelings but in embracing them wholeheartedly?

Imagine you're walking through a forest and suddenly you step upon a thorn that lodges deep into your foot. It's painful, distracting, and all you want is for the discomfort to vanish. So, you reach for the nearest remedy—a numbing agent—and apply it liberally to your wounded foot. Instantly, the pain fades and you continue on your way with the thorn still in your foot but relieved to be free from discomfort.

Numbing pain seems like a simple solution—a quick fix to make the unpleasant sensations go away. Numbing isn't a cure but merely a temporary solution. By numbing our pain, we're not actually solving the problem but masking it, allowing it to fester beneath the surface.

As you continue walking with the thorn in your foot, though the pain is gone, a deep, nasty infection is beginning to form—unbeknownst to you.

When we numb our pain—whether it's physical or emotional—we're essentially silencing the signals that something is wrong without addressing the underlying issue. While we have dulled our perception of the pain, the damage beneath the surface continues to expand. Sure, we might feel better for a while, but eventually, the problem will resurface, often in a more severe form. Just like any temporary solution, numbing comes with its own set of consequences.

When we numb our emotions, we disconnect from our inner selves. We deny ourselves the opportunity to understand what we're truly feeling and why we feel that way. In doing so, we create a void within ourselves—a void that anxiety eagerly fills. Anxiety thrives in the absence of understanding and acceptance. It feeds on our uncertainties and thrives in the shadows of our unacknowledged emotions.

Think of our emotions as messengers delivering important insights about our experiences and needs. When we numb them, we silence these messengers, leaving ourselves in the dark about our own inner workings. And as any darkness goes, it breeds fear and uncertainty.

Consider a woman who's been taught to suppress her anger because society tells her that anger isn't "ladylike." Instead of expressing her frustration, she buries it deep within herself, pretending that everything is fine. But beneath the surface, her suppressed anger simmers, gradually morphing into anxiety. She becomes irritable, constantly on edge, her body tense with the effort of keeping her emotions in check.

Or think of a mother who's expected to be the epitome of selflessness, always putting her family's needs above her own. She ignores her own desires and dreams, pushing them aside in favor of fulfilling her roles as caregiver and nurturer. Yet, deep down, resentment festers, gnawing away at her sense of self. She feels trapped, suffocated by the weight of her unspoken emotions, and anxiety becomes her constant companion.

The truth is, numbing our emotions doesn't make them disappear. Instead, they fester beneath the surface, manifesting as anxiety, depression, or other mental health issues. But there is another way—a way to break free from this cycle of suppression and reclaim our emotional well-being.

It begins with courage—the courage to embrace our vulnerability, sit with our discomfort, and listen to what our emotions are trying to tell us. It means allowing ourselves to feel deeply, even when it's painful, knowing that in doing so we're honoring our own humanity.

It also requires compassion for ourselves and for others. We must learn to treat ourselves with the same kindness and understanding that we would offer to a dear friend. We must recognize that experiencing difficult emotions is a natural part of being human and that we are worthy of love and acceptance no matter what we're feeling.

And finally, it involves connection—reaching out to others and sharing our struggles and triumphs open and honestly. In doing so, we realize that we're not alone, that we're part of a vast tapestry of human experiences woven together by our shared vulnerabilities and strengths.

Numbing pain is directly related to anxiety because even though you can't *feel* your pain anymore, it is still there. And your body knows it.

The anxiety is there to remind you that you still need to deal with the pain. The anxiety is like a flag runner waving that flag high and yelling at you, "HEY! You're not going to ignore this problem! You might not feel it right now, but it is still here! Even though you're numbing it, it's still fucking here. I'm going to create this anxiety so you don't forget about the problem!"

Pain pushes us to do things that we *know* we need to do but would never do otherwise. When we numb our pain, we don't take the actions that pain came to remind us of. Instead, pain sends in its friend anxiety to remind us that pain is still there.

So often when we are in pain we want to rush through the pain and get to the numbing agent as quickly as possible.

While we're numb, we try to hurry and create memories and capture moments before the pain enters again so that we can stay numb longer before the pain comes back. It's like we try to gather nuggets of good times while trying to make happy memories.

While going through my phone once, I saw my iPhone had pulled up one of those automated movies it had created from a moment of my life. This movie happened to be from years before when I was in a former relationship. As I watched the video, I saw there were more than twenty pictures of seemingly incredibly happy moments. If you were watching it as a bystander you would have thought, *Oh what a beautiful family you guys have*. As I watched the video, grief and doubt entered into my heart. Had my life really been as bad as I'd thought it was? Had I sensationalized parts that weren't that good? And then I realized the opposite had happened. I had sensationalized the parts that were good. I would take pictures of those moments, hoping that by capturing the feeling or the moment, the good would last. I was trying to "trap" the moment and feeling because I knew it wouldn't always be there.

You can take photos all day of smiling faces and pretty places, but if you are numbing between the moments of pain, you are not able to truly experience or feel anything.

Are we looking to make moments *look* magical, so we have to take pictures to trick ourselves into believing those moments actually *were* magical? When you're truly happy, you may find you take way fewer pictures.

How often are you taking pictures of seemingly happy moments simply to trick yourself into believing that reality is different than what it is?

Are you cultivating the counterfeit so you can survive the pain?

Numbing not only decreases our ability to feel our pain but also our joy, creativity, and deeper levels of connection with others. It robs us of the full range of human experiences, leaving us feeling disconnected from ourselves and the world around us.

So, what's the solution? Instead of numbing your pain, try leaning into it. Allow yourself to feel your emotions fully, even if they're uncomfortable. Recognize that pain is a natural part of life and that by acknowledging it you can begin to address the root causes of your anxiety. Seek support from loved ones or a professional therapist who can help you navigate your feelings and develop healthier coping mechanisms.

The next time you're tempted to numb your pain—whether it's with alcohol, drugs, or distractions—pause and ask yourself: am I truly solving the problem, or am I just avoiding it? Remember, numbing your pain might provide temporary relief, but it's not a sustainable solution. By embracing your emotions and facing your pain head-on, you can break free from the cycle of anxiety and reclaim your emotional well-being, paving the way for genuine growth and transformation.

HERE ARE SOME POSSIBLE WAYS WE NUMB OUR PAIN:

- **Overworking**: Some women bury themselves in work, taking on excessive responsibilities and tasks to distract themselves from underlying emotional pain. By constantly staying busy, they avoid confronting their feelings and the discomfort that comes with them.
- **Emotional eating:** Turning to food for comfort is a common coping mechanism for many women. Whether it's indulging in sugary snacks or binging on unhealthy foods, emotional eating

provides a temporary escape from emotional distress but ultimately perpetuates a cycle of numbing and guilt.

- **Substance abuse**: Alcohol, drugs, or prescription medications can offer temporary relief from emotional pain. Women may turn to substances to numb their feelings, seeking solace in the altered states of consciousness the substances provide. However, reliance on substances can lead to addiction and exacerbate underlying mental health issues.

- **Distracting behaviors**: Constantly scrolling through social media, binge-watching TV shows, or obsessively shopping online are all ways women may distract themselves from their emotional pain. These behaviors offer a temporary reprieve from discomfort but ultimately prevent women from addressing the root causes of their pain.

- **Pretending everything is fine**: Many women put on a brave face and pretend that everything is okay, even when they're struggling internally. They may suppress their emotions and put on a façade of happiness to avoid burdening others or appearing weak. However, this façade only serves to deepen their sense of isolation and disconnection from themselves and others.

- **Engaging in toxic relationships**: Some women numb their pain by seeking validation and approval from toxic or abusive relationships. They may cling to partners who mistreat them or constantly seek out validation from others, believing that external validation will fill the void within themselves. However, these relationships only perpetuate feelings of worthlessness and inadequacy.

- **Ignoring physical symptoms**: Women may ignore physical symptoms of stress or illness, dismissing them as insignificant or attributing them to other causes. By neglecting their physical health, they avoid confronting the underlying emotional pain that may be contributing to their symptoms.

- **Self-harm**: In extreme cases, women may resort to self-harming behaviors as a way to cope with emotional pain. Cutting, burning, or other forms of self-injury provide a temporary release from overwhelming emotions but can lead to serious physical and psychological consequences.

These examples illustrate the various ways women may numb their pain daily as they seek temporary relief from emotional distress, but the numbing ultimately perpetuates a cycle of avoidance and disconnection. It's important for women to recognize these patterns and seek healthier ways of coping with their emotions, such as therapy, mindfulness practices, and building a supportive network of family and friends.

You have the power to choose to sit with your pain and let it teach you. Let your pain show you exactly where you need to focus your healing. You have the power to rise when the pain is suffocating. You have the power to put the numbing gel down and have the grit to face your pain. There is no way *out* of pain—there is only through—and I know you have the power and resilience to move through pain and rid your life of the by-product of numbing—anxiety.

CHAPTER 26

BURNING THE ALTAR

As I lay quietly in a transformative reiki session, the metaphor of altars and sacrifices unfolded before me like a vivid tapestry, woven with threads of societal norms and personal choices. It struck me deeply: were we, as individuals, unwittingly constructing altars of sacrifice that bind us with invisible chains? Were we surrendering ourselves to patterns of self-imposed slavery without even realizing it?

In that sacred reiki session, I saw a whole lineage of women dutifully approaching their altars, each day sacrificing a piece of themselves. For centuries, they had followed this path that was built upon expectations and passed down through generations. Yet, one day, as I stood before my own altar, I dared to question its purpose. "Why am I doing this?" I wondered aloud, startling those around me who had grown accustomed to the rituals of sacrifice.

With a heart heavy with realization, I made a bold choice: to ignite my altar in fire. This act of defiance against tradition was met with panic and disapproval from those who couldn't fathom such a radical departure from the norm. But for me, it was a necessary act of liberation, a declaration that I would no longer sacrifice my authenticity and autonomy for the sake of conformity.

But among the ashes of my burned altar, I found hope—a hope born of reclaiming my own power and sovereignty. I realized that empowerment isn't about giving away my power to others; it's about showing others how to find their own. It's about breaking free from the chains of societal conditioning and forging a new path based on authenticity and self-discovery.

The journey of dismantling my personal altar of sacrifice wasn't without its challenges. I faced skepticism and resistance, both from within myself and from those around me who couldn't understand my newfound resolve. Yet, in that moment of burning away the old, I discovered a profound truth: true empowerment comes from within. It's about recognizing our own strengths, abilities, and inherent worth independent of social expectations or traditions passed down unquestioned.

The concept of the altar, traditionally associated with religious or spiritual practices, took on a new meaning as I delved deeper into its symbolism. An altar, in its essence, is a place of offering—a sacred space where sacrifices are made in exchange for something greater. But what happens when these altars are not erected in temples or churches but rather within the confines of our own lives? What happens when the sacrifices we make are not to appease gods or deities but to conform to societal expectations and norms?

Reflecting on the sacrifices made by countless women before me, I saw the patterns of self-denial and self-betrayal that had become ingrained in our collective consciousness. We had become adept at constructing altars not just of stone and mortar but of beliefs and behaviors that constrained rather than liberated us.

The journey to reclaiming our power begins with awareness—the awareness that we are not bound by the expectations of others but are free to define our own paths and narratives. It requires courage—the courage to challenge outdated norms and beliefs, to question the validity of the altars we've erected, and to embrace our true selves unapologetically.

I couldn't help but draw parallels between personal stories and broader societal narratives. How many of us have found ourselves sacrificing our dreams, desires, and even our sense of self on the altars of societal expectations? How many of us have willingly surrendered our authenticity in pursuit of acceptance and validation from others?

I thought of the countless women who have been conditioned to believe that their worth is contingent upon their ability to fulfill predefined roles and expectations—whether as the perfect wife, mother, or career woman. I thought of the sacrifices they make every day, often without even realizing it, in the name of duty, obligation, and societal pressure.

But what struck me most was the realization that many of us, myself included, had become complicit in our own subjugation. We had become adept at constructing altars of sacrifice, convinced that they were the only path to fulfillment and success. We had willingly traded our authenticity for the illusion of security and belonging, unaware that we were shackling ourselves to chains of our own making.

In diving deeper into the concept of altars of sacrifice, I began to see them not just as physical constructs but as a symbolic representation of the ways we sacrifice pieces of ourselves in service to society. These altars, invisible yet palpable, exist within the confines of our minds and hearts, shaping our thoughts, beliefs, and behaviors in subtle yet profound ways.

Consider the woman who sacrifices her ambitions and dreams in pursuit of the elusive ideal of perfection—a sacrifice made on the altar of societal pressure to conform to traditional gender roles. She may suppress her own desires and aspirations, believing that her worth is contingent upon her ability to meet external standards of success and achievement.

Or think of the mother who sacrifices her own well-being for the sake of her family—a sacrifice made on the altar of selflessness and martyrdom. She may neglect her own needs and desires, prioritizing the needs of others above her own, all in the name of duty and obligation.

And what about the woman who sacrifices her authenticity and voice in order to fit in and be accepted—a sacrifice made on the altar of social conformity and validation? She may silence her own truths and convictions, contorting herself into the mold prescribed by society, afraid to stand out or rock the boat.

These altars of sacrifice, though constructed with the best of intentions, ultimately serve to imprison us in a cycle of self-denial and self-betrayal. They rob us of our agency, autonomy, and sense of self-worth, leaving us feeling empty, disconnected, and unfulfilled.

It was a sobering realization—one that filled me with both sorrow and hope: sorrow for the countless moments lost to self-imposed bondage but hope for the possibility of liberation and transformation. Because here's the thing: just as we have the power to build these altars, so, too, do we have the power to tear them down. Just as we have sacrificed ourselves, we have the power to reclaim our sovereignty and agency, to redefine our own paths and narratives on our own terms.,

The journey to freedom begins with awareness—the awareness that we are not beholden to societal expectations or norms, that we have the power to redefine our own paths and narratives. It requires courage—the courage to challenge the status quo, to question the validity of the altars we've constructed, and to forge new paths based on our own truths and values, even if they diverge from the expectations imposed upon us by society.

It also requires a willingness to cultivate self-awareness and self-compassion—to acknowledge the ways we've sacrificed ourselves and to forgive ourselves for doing so. It's about recognizing that we are worthy of love and acceptance simply by virtue of our existence, and that our worth is not contingent upon our ability to meet external standards of success or achievement.

And perhaps most importantly, it requires solidarity—the solidarity of women standing together, supporting one another in our quest for liberation and self-discovery. For it is only through collective action and mutual empowerment that we can dismantle the altars of sacrifice and build a world where authenticity, freedom, and self-expression reign supreme.

So let us break free from the chains that bind us. Let us reclaim our power and sovereignty. Let us burn down the altars of sacrifice and forge a new legacy—one of liberation, authenticity, and unapologetic selfhood.

CHAPTER 27

SPIRITUAL TRANSFORMATION

I was terrified to question my own beliefs. I was not looking to have a faith "crisis," as some call it. At the time, I was content in my religion, holding prestigious callings and being deeply involved in the community. But despite my efforts to maintain belief, I found myself unable to reconcile with certain core principles and doctrines. Stepping into questioning my faith and beliefs was terrifying and unsettling. I did not seek reasons to leave a church I was otherwise happy in, but I had to remain true to myself and acknowledge that I did not authentically believe in some fundamental teachings.

One significant moment in this journey occurred during a conversation with a respected business friend who challenged my perspective on religion. This friend, whom I admired for his success and analytical approach to business, posed a thought-provoking question one evening at the dinner table when we were discussing the religion we both belonged to.

"Robyn," he began, "when you start a business, what's the first thing you do?"

"I research other businesses like it and study how they are successful. I find their history. I study my competitors," I replied confidently, reflecting on my thorough approach to business ventures.

He paused, then continued, "I'm surprised you follow this religion so closely without doing any research about it, about its history and origin. Do you truly understand the religion you are so committed to?"

I was taken back and quite offended he would say this.

His words struck a chord within me. It was the first time someone had challenged my beliefs in such a direct manner. I found myself pondering deeply: Did I actually believe in the religion I was so committed to? Had I truly studied its history and doctrines? Did I genuinely understand what I was practicing and professing?

This conversation became a catalyst for introspection and self-examination. It sparked a journey of questioning and seeking deeper understanding—a journey that eventually led me to reevaluate my beliefs and redefine my spiritual path.

Another significant moment in my journey of questioning faith occurred when it was time to baptize my firstborn into the church I belonged to. At the age of eight, my daughter was eager and excited for her big day, which is traditionally celebrated with a white dress, delicious brunch, and celebration. As I watched her prepare for baptism, I couldn't help but notice her innocence and youthfulness. She still believed in Santa Claus, and I wondered how she could possess the mental and emotional maturity to commit her life to a religion at such a tender age.

During this time of preparation, my thoughts turned to the ordinance associated with baptism—receiving the gift of the Holy Ghost. According to teachings in my faith, after baptism, a worthy priesthood holder lays his hands on the child's head and bestows upon them the gift of the Holy Ghost. The Holy Ghost is believed to be a constant companion that enables individuals to know the truth of all things. It was taught to be a sacred witness and the person is promised the continual presence of the Holy Ghost, a member of the Godhead.

However, as I reflected on this ritual, a realization dawned upon me—I didn't believe in this concept as it was taught. I couldn't reconcile the idea that this gift was exclusive to those baptized in a specific faith. I believed that every individual is born with the inherent right to the constant companionship of the Holy Ghost, regardless of religious affiliation or ceremonial rites. To me, this divine connection wasn't conditional upon baptism or perfect adherence to religious rules. It is a birthright, a spiritual birthright accessible to all.

This moment was pivotal in my journey of questioning and reevaluating my beliefs. It marked a profound shift in my understanding of spirituality and the nature of divine connection. I realized that my spiritual path was leading me toward a more inclusive and expansive understanding of faith—one that transcended the confines of organized religion and embraced a broader spectrum of spiritual experiences.

Leaving a religion I once believed to be the one true path was a devastating realization. It wasn't just about leaving behind doctrines and teachings; it meant potentially losing friends, family, and the entire community that had been a cornerstone of my life. The thought of unsettling my family, upending my lifestyle, and facing the disapproval of those I loved was daunting.

I grappled with a profound choice—continue in the religion to maintain family and community harmony, despite my growing doubts and inner conflict, or stay true to myself and honor the truth I was discovering within. The pressure to conform, to silence my doubts and questions, was immense. I was taught that questioning the church was akin to being influenced by the adversary, a path leading *away* from God's truth.

Yet, deep within, I knew that authenticity required honesty with myself. Could I continue to suppress my doubts and beliefs simply to avoid disrupting the status quo? Or was I being called to trust my intuition, even if it meant facing the unknown and potential isolation?

Amid the anxiety and uncertainty, I found solace in trusting my own inner guidance. I embarked on a journey of self-discovery and spiritual exploration, guided by a sense of integrity and authenticity. I learned to navigate the complexities of faith and identity with compassion for myself and understanding for those around me.

This journey was not without challenges. It required courage to confront deeply ingrained beliefs and societal expectations. It demanded vulnerability to acknowledge and honor my evolving spiritual truth, even in the face of resistance or misunderstanding from others.

Ultimately, I chose to embrace the unsettling process of questioning and redefining my beliefs. It was a journey toward greater personal freedom and spiritual authenticity where I discovered that my connection with the Divine transcends any institutional framework or religious dogma.

To those who find solace and meaning within organized religion, I extend my deepest respect and understanding. Your faith journey is valid and significant, shaped by personal experiences and spiritual convictions that deserve reverence. I recognize the strength and comfort that community and tradition can provide, offering a sense of belonging and purpose that enriches lives in profound ways.

For those within organized religion who may question or experience doubt, I offer solidarity and empathy. Your journey of faith is uniquely yours, and it's okay to wrestle with uncertainties and seek deeper understanding. Trust in your inner wisdom and the guidance of your heart as you navigate the complexities of belief and spirituality.

Let my experience be a testament to the transformative power of questioning, exploration, and spiritual freedom. It celebrates the courage to challenge beliefs, the strength to embrace flexibility, and the joy of discovering spiritual truths that resonate deeply within our souls.

May this journey be a source of inspiration and empowerment for you as you navigate your own path of spiritual exploration. May you find solace in knowing that your connection with the Divine is a deeply personal and intimate experience, one that invites you to question, explore, and embrace the boundless possibilities of your own spiritual journey.

Together, let us walk hand in hand toward a deeper understanding of ourselves and the divine presence that dwells within and around us.

I challenge you to contemplate the idea that stepping away from organized religion does not diminish the depth of your spiritual journey. Instead, it opens doors to a more personal, intimate relationship with the Divine. Know that my love for God extends to you, reassuring you that you are deeply cherished and supported on your path of spiritual exploration.

As we embark on this journey together, it's essential to honor the paths that others choose, including those who find solace and spiritual fulfillment within organized religion. For many, the structure, community, and rituals offered by religious institutions provide a sense of belonging and spiritual nourishment. These institutions have historically served as pillars of support and guidance for countless individuals seeking deeper connection with the Divine.

While my journey led me away from traditional religious frameworks, I recognize and respect that each person's path is unique. The diversity of spiritual practices and beliefs enriches our collective understanding of the Divine and contributes to the tapestry of human spirituality. Whether one finds God in the rituals of a church, the serenity of meditation, or the communion of nature, each expression is valid and deserving of reverence.

Embracing diversity in spiritual expression is one of the most profound lessons I have learned.

In embracing flexibility in our spiritual beliefs, we celebrate the diverse ways in which people connect with the Divine. Just as the river flows through varied landscapes, so, too, does spirituality weave through different cultures, traditions, and personal experiences. Our capacity to evolve and adapt spiritually allows us to appreciate the richness of these diverse expressions without feeling confined to any single path or doctrine.

By embracing this diversity, we honor the essence of spiritual exploration as a deeply personal and transformative journey. It is a journey that invites us to explore beyond the boundaries of what we have been taught, to question assumptions, and to discover our own truths about the nature of existence and our place within it.

Ultimately, the essence of spirituality lies in love and compassion. Regardless of our religious affiliations or spiritual practices, these universal principles unite us in our shared humanity. Love transcends doctrinal differences, offering a common ground where empathy and understanding can flourish.

As we navigate the complexities of spiritual exploration, let us hold space for each other's beliefs with kindness and respect. Let us listen with open hearts, recognizing that our paths may diverge, but our quest for spiritual fulfillment unites us in a shared pursuit of meaning and connection.

CHAPTER 28

BADGE OF HONOR

Our "badge of honor" will become our children's trauma. The concept of wearing a badge of honor for enduring suffering has been deeply ingrained in many of us. However, true honor doesn't lie in how long we hold onto a particular truth but in our courage to let it evolve. Embracing change and growth is an anthem for our resilience and a celebration of our journey.

When we are not strong enough to uphold our boundaries, we flip the narrative. Every time he returns to his mistress or indulges in unhealthy habits, we wear his actions as our own badge of honor. We stay and justify our choices by saying *we love him*; *it's for the kids*; or *it's because we're good people*. But these justifications are lies, and that badge of honor is nothing to be proud of.

How often do we hold the pain and the responsibility for someone else? When we don't allow people we love to take accountability, we're essentially robbing them of the joy of personal growth. By shielding them from the consequences of their actions, we deny them the opportunity to experience the full spectrum of life's emotions.

In my former relationship, just like I picked up my partner's clothes and essentially acted as the maid who took care of everything, I also absorbed his parenting responsibilities. This contributed to my former partner being very uninvolved with our kids. He loved them, but he didn't invest time or energy into being a father. This changed after our divorce as being a present father was no longer optional. The divorce, while devastating, also became a catalyst for positive change in his life. Stripped of my enabling role, he had to step up and be a father, spending quality time with the kids and building relationships that would have otherwise been missed. Co-parenting may not be easy for us, but the divorce allowed him to become the dad he is now—a role he might never have embraced if we had stayed married.

Instead of viewing divorce solely as a loss, why not see it as a significant gain? The appreciation I have for my children now surpasses anything I felt before. When you are the primary caregiver, and in the snap of a finger fifty percent of your children's lives are no longer spent with you, you begin to view your role differently. This abrupt shift compels you to use your time more intentionally when you have your children.

Before the divorce, I loved my children deeply, but the difference now is that I cherish every waking moment with them. I do not let a day go by without focusing on the immense gratitude I feel for being their mother. Divorce has also provided a unique opportunity for my children to witness their mother stepping into her power. They have seen me rise from the ashes, more resilient and stronger than ever.

Though the journey of divorce has been more tragic than I can express in words, I now recognize the blessings it has brought into my life and the lives of my children. This experience has taught us invaluable lessons about strength, resilience, and the importance of cherishing every moment. Divorce, while challenging, has allowed us to grow individually and collectively, creating a deeper, more meaningful bond.

In many ways, this transformation has been a blessing in disguise. It has provided a platform for me to demonstrate to my children the importance of self-respect, personal growth, and the courage to make difficult decisions for the betterment of our lives. They have seen firsthand the power of perseverance and the beauty of finding joy and gratitude in the present moment.

I choose to focus on the positive aspects of our journey. I choose to see divorce not as an end, but as a beginning—a beginning of a new chapter filled with appreciation, intentionality, and a deeper love for my children. This perspective has enriched our lives and allowed us to move forward with hope and strength, embracing the future with open hearts and minds.

Divorce is often viewed through a lens of taboo, with society focusing on the negative aspects: the loss, the heartbreak, the perceived failure. But my children and I have experienced a different narrative. Despite the stigma surrounding my divorce, our journey has been one of profound growth and transformation. We have faced our challenges head-on and emerged stronger and more connected than ever before.

People often concentrate on the hardships and overlook the potential for personal development and newfound strength that can arise from such a life-changing event. Through this process, my children and I have learned to adapt, to support one another, and to find joy in our new circumstances. We've discovered the importance of resilience and the power of choosing to see the positive in every situation.

By breaking free from the constraints of societal expectations and embracing our reality, we have created a life filled with intentionality and gratitude. Our story is a testament to the fact that, even in the face of adversity, there is always room for growth and the possibility of a brighter future.

Our badge of honor should not become our children's trauma. The true honor lies in teaching them resilience, strength, and self-love.

We have the power to create a new narrative, one in which we honor our truths, embrace change, and celebrate our journeys. It's time to let go of the false badges of honor and step into a life of authenticity and empowerment. We owe it to ourselves and to the generations that follow.

CHAPTER 29

THE MODEST WOMAN

I can't give you my power, but I can help you find yours. Empowering another woman isn't about handing over my strength; it's about helping you discover your own. True empowerment comes from within and involves recognizing and embracing your own potential. It's a journey of self-awareness, accountability, and personal growth. Empowerment isn't something borrowed; it's something earned through your own efforts. As we uplift others, we create a collective strength that lifts us all. Your power is unique, and when you embrace it, you contribute to a more inclusive and supportive world for all women.

Empowering others is a natural extension of living in your own power. It involves mentoring, supporting, and inspiring others to cultivate their unique strengths and abilities. By sharing our journeys and leading by example, we create a ripple effect of empowerment that uplifts entire communities.

As you step into your power, it's important to remember that empowerment isn't just about what you achieve or how loudly you assert yourself—it's also reflected in how you choose to present yourself to the world. Modesty in dress is a form of empowerment that allows you to express your identity with dignity and self-respect. It's not about hiding who you are but about owning your worth and choosing to showcase it on your terms. The way we dress can be a powerful statement of our values, our self-respect, and our inner strength.

I still remember a conversation with my sister as clearly as the day it happened. We were walking on a paved leisure trail and I was asking her questions about why she had recently left organized religion.

I was asking her so I could judge her for why she wasn't wearing her religious garments anymore. I wanted to know. I wanted to debate her poor decision to no longer wear them. I was acting as if I was curious, but I was going to wait for her to say something and then I was going to rebut.

When I started asking her about why she wasn't wearing her religious garments, she made a point that I had never heard before. "I don't wear them anymore, but not for the reasons that we would all think. I feel like [they are] a suppression of feminism. I feel like it's a way that they put these clothes on us: they're to our knees, [over] our shoulders. It feels like a way to suppress me because power comes from my sensuality. And if they can suppress my sexual side, my powerful side, then I have no power in all the other ways."

I was hard core judging her while simultaneously feeling intrigued, so I asked her to share more with me. She explained that when she decided to no longer wear her garments, she was in control of her body and could now show shoulders, legs, and stomach without it being sexualized at all. She expressed, "I've never felt more empowered. It's a way to make women feel less powerful. To hide and cover up. To feel shame and insecurity in showing parts of us. But when I took them off, I realized religion wants you to think that the power is within the religion, not within yourself. If everyone walked around knowing *they* were the power, there wouldn't be religion because we wouldn't need it."

It sparked a snowball effect in my mind about how I viewed my body and my own inner power, which had been completely suppressed. I used to view my sensual side as dark and unnecessary, but now, I see a woman who feels more empowered than ever. My inner essence is one of my most powerful parts.

I believe it is time for women to awaken their sensuality. Many women avoid talking or reading about it because we carry so much shame and guilt around the topic. We're afraid of being perceived as provocative or immodest.

However, modesty doesn't mean suppressing sensuality. Embracing your sensuality—whether in your body, your sexuality, or how you choose to show your body—is part of honoring who you are. There is no guilt or shame in feeling comfortable in your own skin and expressing your sensuality. Sensuality is not just about sex; it's about being fully alive in your body, appreciating its beauty, and allowing yourself the freedom to feel and express pleasure. When you own your sensuality without fear or shame, you claim another facet of your power—one that is deeply connected to self-love, confidence, and true liberation.

What does your definition of modesty mean? Mine has evolved as I've expanded.

For me, Modesty is simply about *intention.*

> *If I wear something with the intention of provoking someone else's husband, then I'm being immodest.*
> *If I purposefully wear something to attract attention from another man, that's being immodest.*
> *If I wear something to get others to stare at me, that's being immodest.*

But if I'm wearing my bikini in Hawaii, and my intention has nothing to do with seeing if other men will look at me while I'm wearing it, then it is modest. Wearing a bikini can still be modest if it comes from a place of self-love and comfort. It's all about my *mindset* and *intention* when I put it on. Personally, I've experienced a lot of guilt and shame while unraveling modesty and my original beliefs I was raised with. When I stopped wearing my religious garments, modesty as I knew it changed.

I believe modesty is your INTENTION, not the actual style or length of the clothing.

Modesty is fundamentally tied to our inner motivations and the messages we wish to convey through our appearance. Clothing, while often seen as an external factor, is a powerful medium of expression that reflects our internal state. When we choose to dress ourselves, the intention behind our choices speaks volumes about our sense of self-respect, confidence, and the values we hold.

Self-love and comfort are central to the concept of modesty. When we dress in a way that makes us feel good and aligns with our personal comfort, we are honoring ourselves. This self-respect radiates outward, projecting an image of confidence and authenticity. Conversely, when clothing choices are driven by a desire to attract inappropriate attention or to compete with others, we compromise our integrity and shift away from true modesty.

Modesty is a personal journey and a reflection of our inner values and intentions. It's about dressing in a way that aligns with who we are and what we believe in, rather than conforming to societal standards or seeking validation from others. When our intention is to express self-love, respect for others, and a true representation of our identity, we embody modesty regardless of the specific clothing we wear.

This perspective on modesty encourages us to shift the focus from external judgments to internal motivations. It challenges us to consider why we wear certain things and to ensure they reflect our authentic selves. By doing so, we can embrace a form of modesty that is empowering, respectful, and true to our personal values.

CHAPTER 30

THE GATHERER

When I was a child, finding friends came very naturally to me. I was outgoing, willing to pursue new friends at the local neighborhood park, and always treated my close friends with kindness and care. The majority of my childhood friends stayed close until we got into junior high. This is where the process of "natural hot girl selection" started to change our friendships. I unfortunately didn't make the cut and watched my best friends become the school's most popular girls while I took the back seat.

I was left out of hangouts and not invited to parties. I was a total loser because I hadn't been encouraged by my parents to wear makeup and designer clothes and my boobs hadn't come in. Junior high and the beginning of high school were the most difficult years of adolescence I can recall. I was made fun of, left out, and gossiped about. I'm honestly shocked I made it through.

I finally realized the secret to becoming popular and liked wasn't what I wore, how many boys liked me, or if I had boobs. I found the secret antidote: being myself fully. I became noticed, liked, and ultimately super popular in high school simply because I was funny, kind, goofy, and made people laugh. I didn't have a nice car, a nice body, nice clothes, or a boyfriend. I simply showed up as the honest, quirky, and hilarious version of Robyn. IT WORKED!

This served me well into my last two years of high school. I had friends in every clique and didn't have the typical friend drama most people had in high school. My high school years were so good to me in the friend department. I had more friends than I can remember and all my memories were amazing. I never had a friend breakup, or honestly even any drama. Most of my high school friends I am still very close with to this day.

Those friends stayed with me into my early years of marriage. We still all lived in the hometown we grew up in. Outside of hanging out with my mom and sisters, my high school friends remained my constants.

It wasn't until I was twenty-nine and built a house in a town twenty-five minutes away that I learned about the complexities, nuances, and straight up JUNGLE it could be to find and navigate adult relationships. Unlike the structured environments of our youth, where friendships naturally flourished at school or in our neighborhoods, adulthood demands intentional effort to forge and maintain connections. While childhood friendships often blossom effortlessly, adulthood presents challenges that can strain even the strongest bonds.

As I moved into my neighborhood, I realized the importance and urgency of making new friends where I lived. I could not rely on my high school friends as much because kids and busy lives made it more difficult to get together. I went to work and decided to start putting energy into finding new friends.

What I didn't know, however, was the danger adult friendships could bring if you happened to make them with the wrong group. To make a long story short, I found myself in the local "ward clique." For those not familiar with the LDS culture, a "ward" is a group of Mormons who all live near each other and attend the same congregation.

These ladies in my ward were fun, kind, and accepting—at first. I quickly learned the social hierarchy in the friend group. I realized there was a set of unspoken rules and I was the first to break one when I found myself connecting with one of the women in the group. She and I hit it off quickly and had so much in common. We loved hanging out and our kids quickly became besties. I didn't realize that this was against the group rules because she was already "someone else's best friend."

To summarize this story, it was the wild wild west of friend groups. Some of the ladies in the group went out of their way to make my life a living hell because of my infectious, happy personality. They immediately felt threatened by and jealous of my ability to be welcomed into the group so quickly. Other members of the group liked me and started to hang out with me outside of the group's "sanctioned events."

A few of the ladies who did not approve of me becoming "popular" in the group started making up insane lies and rumors about my new "best friend" and me. They even went as far as trying to get our local bishop and stake president (local church government) involved. When they brought our husbands into the mess, I knew I had to get out quickly.

Gossip and drama have a notorious reputation for sowing seeds of discord and mistrust, wreaking havoc on friendships. In a culture that thrives on sensationalism and scandal, it was all too easy to get swept up in the allure of gossip, spreading rumors, and negativity without considering the consequences. It had only been six short months since I had moved in, but I knew this group of women was up to no good and completely toxic. Though I was desperate to fit in and have friends, I knew it was better to be alone than join their bad behavior.

I remember the first time I ever said "fuck" was at a meeting the friend "leader" had arranged. She invited us all to her home to discuss the drama SHE and others had been creating. I was hesitant to even go, but they had such a way of bullying and creating problems that I wanted to know what was being said.

I sat there and heard every woman stand up to state their "case" and address the rumors and gossip. As I awaited my turn, I wanted to throw up in my mouth because of how dramatic and disappointing these women were. The "meeting" got so out of control, and knowing I could no longer associate myself with these types of women, I stood up and shouted, "NEVER SAY MY FUCKING NAME OUT OF YOUR MOUTH AGAIN! NEVER COME TO MY HOME! NEVER SEND YOUR CHILDREN EITHER! NEVER START ANOTHER RUMOR OR LIE ABOUT ME! NEVER. SAY. MY. FUCKING. NAME. OUT. OF YOUR. MOUTH. AGAIN! I WANT NOTHING TO DO WITH ANY OF YOU!"

The Gatherer

As I stormed out of the front door, adrenaline rushed through my body and tears filled my eyes. I vowed to NEVER have another friend experience like this again. Looking back, I could have handled the situation better, but standing my ground with a virgin F-word felt like the right move.

Since that day, I have never associated with, hung out with, or invited these women over to my house (though I've offered a friendly "hello" in passing). It's been eight years, and we live in the same neighborhood. It was the most traumatic friendship experience of my adult life.

I knew I had to forge my own path of adult friendships and find a way to custom-create a group of women I felt safe with. I didn't want to feel chained to only hanging out with women who lived close by, as clearly the options I had were not healthy at the time. I was too far from my sisters and high school friends and totally wounded and traumatized from my first attempt at making adult friends. Is this how it was with everyone? Was everyone experiencing the same thing?

I've spent the past eight years promising to do it differently and make having adult friendships a safe experience for women. I was so focused on this passion of "no woman left behind" that I ended up creating an entire social group and business dedicated to hosting a safe environment for women to find their *ComeUNITY*.

I learned I have a special gift of gathering. This became especially prevalent in 2019 when I discovered my "word" for my New Year's resolution. Instead of choosing goals like, "lose ten pounds," or "run a marathon," I decided to choose a word I wanted to focus on for the year. I ultimately landed on "gather." What I wrote down was:

GATHER

> Gather my family around the dinner table each night (I wanted to make dinner and eat as a family more often).
> Gather people to find and choose God (I wanted to share my testimony of God more often).
> Gather my friends in my home (I wanted to invite people over to my home more often, as it was something that had given me anxiety in the past).
> Gather my talents and focus on those (I wanted to focus on my talents and build business around them).

Gather . . . the list went on.

I never realized how significant my new role as "the gatherer" would be.

In my quest to find a safe and happy friend group, I found myself in a dilemma. I still had friend cliques I cherished, but I always felt torn on which ones to commit my time and limited available Fridays too. I had my high school friends, my childhood friends, my college roommates, my employees (who were all women), my neighborhood friends, my dance mom friends, my kids' friends' moms. . . . What happened when one or more of them wanted to get together or do a girls trip?

I decided to try something that I hadn't seen done before. I fully stepped into my role as the gatherer. This meant I could introduce my college roommates to my neighbors and help them to become friends. This meant I could host a neighborhood party and invite my childhood friends. This meant I could host a girls vacation and have my high school friends hang out with my children's friends' moms. Guess what? It worked!

Relatively quickly, my social gatherings evolved into something magical: a convergence of my dearest friends from various phases of my life, each discovering the brilliance and warmth in one another. It was a deliberate effort that blossomed into a vibrant community. Through this experience, I realized something profound: women crave a tribe, a sanctuary where they can authentically connect and thrive. As the gatherer, this role became intertwined with my purpose—to cultivate safe spaces and foster genuine connections among women within my closest circles and beyond.

One of my most cherished accomplishments has been witnessing these groups of women flourish. To see them not only bond but also support and uplift each other has been a source of immense joy and fulfillment. Creating and nurturing such a community is a rare privilege that requires careful stewardship to maintain its integrity and safety.

Yet, being the gatherer doesn't shield you from challenges. Occasionally, individuals may enter the group with agendas that clash with the group's purpose. They seek gossip or drama instead of genuine connection. I've encountered such instances when someone's intentions didn't align with our values, and they naturally distanced themselves from the group. Maintaining a safe environment requires vigilance and a commitment to the shared vision of authenticity and support.

There have also been times when the role of gatherer has exposed vulnerabilities. Some individuals have taken advantage of my openness in introducing them to my circle as they've exploited those connections for personal gain or excluded me later on. It's a painful lesson that not everyone you invite into your circle will reciprocate your intentions or respect your boundaries.

As a gatherer, it's crucial to recognize these dynamics without losing faith in the power of genuine connections. Those who seek to manipulate or disrupt the harmony of your community will ultimately reveal themselves and depart, despite their efforts to disrupt or divide.

It's important to acknowledge that not every person who crosses your path will be aligned with your mission or values. Some may betray your trust or cause you pain along the way. However, this journey is about resilience and perseverance—to continue seeking and nurturing relationships with women who share your vision of authenticity and mutual support.

Navigating these challenges isn't easy, and there's no guarantee of escaping unscathed. But the rewards of building a community where women feel seen, heard, and valued far outweigh the risks. It's a journey of growth, learning, and empowerment—one that strengthens your resolve and deepens your understanding of the bonds that truly matter.

So, continue marching forward with determination and compassion. Cherish the women who stand beside you, uplift those who share your journey, and trust that through authenticity and resilience, you will cultivate a community where every woman can thrive.

For the greater and most recent part of my adult life, I had a friend who was very dear to me. She was my closest friend and confidant through some of the most painful years of my life. Observers would say we had a power friendship, that we were inseparable and closer than sisters. And she was that for me; I considered her my sister. Our families, lives, and even business were blended together. We spent most of our time with each other and she was truly my closest friend. For eight years, I considered her my other half.

Over the course of a few months, I noticed her becoming distant at times. I was unsure why and had questions about behaviors that I had never seen her exhibit before. As true friends do, we communicated when there was a disagreement or difference of opinions. I checked in frequently and after a handful of conversations about why I could feel her distancing, I felt reassured everything was fine. But it wasn't. After more conversations, she disclosed to me that she was distancing herself because *my* light was too bright. She was telling me this to describe what she wasn't able to communicate: that she was jealous and insecure. *Your light is too bright, Robyn. In order for me to shine as bright as you, I have to step away from you so I can shine on my own.*

Jealousy, rooted in feelings of inadequacy or fear of abandonment, can poison even the most cherished friendships. In a society that often pits women against each other in a constant battle for validation and success, it's easy to succumb to the allure of comparison and envy. Whether it's coveting a friend's achievements, relationships, or lifestyle, jealousy can erode trust and breed resentment if left unchecked. However, recognizing and acknowledging these feelings with honesty and vulnerability can pave the way for healing and deeper connection. By celebrating each other's successes and offering genuine support, we can transform envy into admiration and strengthen our bonds.

You are never too bright for anyone. Seek out women who not only embrace your radiance but also encourage you to shine even brighter. Surround yourself with those whose presence uplifts and inspires you, whose own brilliance ignites a fire within your soul. These are the women whose light doesn't diminish in the face of yours but instead radiates alongside it, amplifying the warmth and strength of your collective glow.

Stand beside women whose brilliance is so palpable that on days when you feel your light flicker, theirs envelops you with its reassuring warmth. Embrace their energy, their wisdom, and their unyielding spirit, for in their presence you find a mirror reflecting the best of who you are and who you can become.

As we each embrace our individual brilliance, we contribute to a collective radiance that brightens the lives of everyone we encounter. It's a synergy where each woman's unique light enhances the whole, creating a tapestry of warmth and illumination that touches hearts and minds alike.

Never allow anyone's jealousy or insecurities to dim your light. Shine boldly, unapologetically, and without reservation. Remember, the sun doesn't apologize for its brilliance; it simply shines, illuminating the world with its undeniable presence. Similarly, your light has the power to inspire, guide, and uplift, so let it shine brightly for yourself *and* for those who bask in its glow.

In the company of bright, empowering women, you find not just camaraderie but a shared journey of growth and empowerment. Together, as we celebrate each other's successes and support each other through challenges, we strengthen the fabric of our collective brilliance. Let us stand together, shining as beacons of hope, resilience, and unwavering strength, lighting the way for a brighter, more radiant future.

Despite our best efforts, some friendships may ultimately come to an end, leaving us grappling with feelings of loss and uncertainty. Whether it's due to irreconcilable differences, betrayal, or simply outgrowing each other, parting ways can be a challenging but necessary step in our personal growth journey. While the process of letting go can be painful and messy, it's essential to honor our feelings and allow ourselves to grieve the loss. By embracing the lessons we've learned and focusing on nurturing relationships that bring joy and fulfillment, we can emerge from the ashes of failed friendships together, stronger, wiser, and more resilient than before.

While the terrain of adult female friendships may be paved with obstacles and challenges, there are certain hallmarks of healthy relationships that serve as beacons of light amid the darkness. Here are the signs I look for in a healthy friendship.

1. **Trust and honesty**: feeling safe to share our thoughts, feelings, and vulnerabilities without fear of judgment or betrayal

2. **Mutual respect**: valuing each other's opinions, boundaries, and autonomy, and treating each other with kindness and consideration

3. **Support and encouragement**: offering emotional support, encouragement, and celebration of each other's successes and achievements

4. **Communication**: open, honest, and respectful communication, even during difficult conversations or conflicts

5. **Shared values and interests**: aligning on core values, interests, and life goals, fostering a sense of connection and camaraderie

Friendships, like any relationship, are subject to change and evolution over time. As we navigate the ebbs and flows of life, it's natural for friends to drift apart or diverge on their paths. While the prospect of losing a friend can be daunting and so painful, it's essential to approach distance with grace and understanding. Instead of clinging to the past or harboring resentment, embrace the opportunity for growth and self-discovery that comes with change. Whether the distance is temporary or permanent, honoring the inherent fluidity of friendships can lead to deeper connections and new beginnings.

Navigating adult female friendships is a journey with twists and turns, triumphs and setbacks. By embracing vulnerability, fostering open communication, and prioritizing mutual respect, we can cultivate deep and meaningful connections that enrich our lives and nourish our souls. Remember that friendship, like any relationship, requires effort, patience, and understanding, but the rewards of authentic connection and companionship are well worth the investment. As we navigate the complexities of adult life, let us cherish the bonds that uplift and inspire us and gracefully release those that no longer serve our highest good. Through it all, may we continue to grow, learn, and evolve, forging a path of love, connection, and authenticity.

CHAPTER 31

DISCOVERING YOUR INNER STRENGTH

Birthing my third child, unmedicated, was the most profound moment I can remember that I realized my innate and divine strength. I always had a desire to have an unmedicated birth. When I was pregnant with my third child, I would watch clips on Instagram of women giving birth unmedicated and I would see their power radiating through my phone.

As I started bringing up this idea to my friends and family, most of the women around me wrote off my idea, saying that I should just get an epidural. Some of them really frowned upon it and said I had nothing to prove. They wondered why I would try now when I had already had two good experiences with epidurals. Why would I intentionally inflict pain on myself when there were drugs to numb it?

I really felt this deep calling inside of me that I wanted to do it unmedicated, and I couldn't find anyone who would champion me. I kind of let it go by the wayside as I progressed in my pregnancy, and I never prepped as those who go unmedicated often do. I never took a hypnobirthing class. I never got a BOSU ball. I didn't know any specific positions. I didn't know how to comfort myself. The most education I had was a knowing that I was capable of doing it. I truly was unprepared, but I had a deep desire to go through childbirth unmedicated.

When I got to the hospital, because I was being induced, the nurse very kindly asked me if I had any sort of delivery plan or expectations. I felt safe with her because she asked me this and I told her I had a deep desire to go unmedicated. I was surprised when she did not talk me out of it and instead said, "Amazing! I know you can totally do it. I have given birth to all my children unmedicated, and I'm going to help you do it."

I immediately felt her power champion and support me in doing something that, honestly, I had not totally thought through. All it took was a moment of her sharing her power and encouraging me to embrace my power. The doctor came in shortly after and the nurse proclaimed, "We are going to do an unmedicated birth." He wasn't super happy about this, and honestly he just wanted me to get the epidural, but he went along with it saying that we could "try."

During the labor, I was overwhelmed by the intensity of the experience. The pain was unlike anything I had ever felt, but so was the profound sense of empowerment. The nurse's unwavering support and belief in me made all the difference. She coached me through each contraction, offering words of encouragement and practical advice on how to manage the pain.

This nurse was so sweet and never made me feel stupid for not having all the tools and gadgets other women bring with them for an unmedicated birth. She sat with me for six hours and helped me labor through. She brought me a BOSU ball and showed me how to use it, her patience and kindness evident in every gesture. She championed me for six hours, reassuring me that I could absolutely do this. In moments when I felt insecure about my plan, she empowered me to keep going, her words a steady source of encouragement.

Unfortunately, her shift ended, and though I felt we had completely bonded, my one warrior left. The next nurse came in, and her tone was completely different. I could sense she was rushed and that I wasn't important to her. When I told her I was going to continue unmedicated, she totally crushed my dreams by saying we would try, but if it became complicated at all, I should get the epidural.

She also encouraged me not to inflict this sort of pain on myself and just use the drug. What she didn't realize was that I wasn't about to inflict pain on myself; I was about to tap into an unfiltered, raw power that I had never felt before. Here was this woman telling me to simply live beneath my potential. Every time my contractions started to get painful and I began to panic, she reminded me to just use the drugs. I was so bothered by how she didn't want me to step into my own power.

In those moments, I realized the stark difference between the two nurses. One saw my strength and encouraged me to embrace it, while the other seemed to undermine my efforts and resilience. It was disheartening to see how quickly my environment shifted from supportive to dismissive. Despite her discouragement, I held onto the memory of the first nurse's unwavering belief in me. I knew that the strength she saw in me was real, and I was determined to find it within myself again no matter how challenging the labor got.

As I got further into the process, I started to become so proud of myself. With each contraction picking up in pace and intensity, I focused on my breath and talked to myself through the pain. In those moments my inner dialogue became a powerful source of strength and encouragement.

Wow, Rob, you're really doing it. I am so proud of you.

I marveled at my own resilience, realizing that despite my initial uncertainty, I was proving to myself just how capable I was.

You totally were unsure if you were capable, but look, you are. What a badass you are. To walk in here with zero plan and nothing more than a desire, and you're doing it. Hell yes!

The acknowledgment of my own bravery and determination fueled me further. I reminded myself to keep breathing, to stay present and focused.

Just keep breathing. This pain won't last forever. Here, let's count till the end of the contraction. We got this.

Counting through the contractions, I found a rhythm, a way to manage the pain and stay grounded. I recognized the enormity of what I was doing, one of the hardest things a woman can do.

You are doing one of the hardest things a woman can do. Keep going. I am so proud of you.

This self-talk became my anchor, reinforcing my strength and resilience. It was a testament to my inner power, a reminder that I was capable of enduring and overcoming. Each contraction was a step closer to my goal, and with every breath, I embraced my own courage and tenacity.

With each contraction I focused on my breath and the voice inside my head, trying to center myself and stay calm. As I progressed, the contractions became more intense and lasted longer. The pain seemed to intensify with every wave, and I started to feel a rising sense of panic. Doubts crept in. Could I really do this? If the pain continued to worsen and the contractions lengthened, did I have the strength to endure it?

I felt maxed out both physically and mentally. My body was tired, and my stamina felt questionable. The effort of maintaining my composure and pushing through the pain was beginning to take its toll. The fear of reaching my limit loomed over me, casting a shadow on my capabilities.

But amid the uncertainty and exhaustion, I tried to hold onto the encouraging voice inside me. It reminded me of my inner strength, urging me to take one breath at a time, one contraction at a time. I needed to trust in my body's ability to handle the process, even when it seemed overwhelming. The pain was intense, but deep down I knew I had to keep going, to find that inner reserve of strength that I hoped was still there.

Again, the voice came into my head.

> *You can do this. Women are made to bring life into this world. Your body knows what to do. Trust yourself. Do not give up. Step into your power and embrace your boldness. You can do this, Robyn.*

I started to sense a presence in the room that I had never felt so strongly before. It was familiar, yet not something I encountered regularly. A feminine, soft, and encouraging being was with me, right next to me, coaching me all along. It was then that I realized the voice encouraging and supporting me was not just my own thoughts. It was the voice of a celestial woman, a divine presence.

My Heavenly Mother had come to me, showing me that I didn't need preparation, protocols, or a plan to access my strength. It was innately there within me, waiting to be discovered. Her presence was like a warm embrace filling me with a sense of peace and reassurance. She taught me that true strength comes from within and that I already possessed everything I needed to overcome this challenge.

In that moment, I understood that my Heavenly Mother had always been with me, guiding and supporting me, even when I wasn't aware of it. Her gentle encouragement had been the source of my resilience and courage. Now, feeling Her presence so vividly, I knew I could deliver this baby with confidence.

When it was finally time to push, I drew on every ounce of strength I had. An indescribable pain entered my body as this precious soul was crowning. The experience was raw and primal, and as I birthed my child, I felt a surge of power and accomplishment that was indescribable. The moment my baby was placed in my arms, I knew that I had tapped into a well of inner strength I didn't fully realize I possessed. I had met the most empowered version of myself as well as sat with my Heavenly Mother.

During those intense final moments, an innate trust in my own body emerged. I had to surrender to the natural process and let my body do what it was designed to do. This trust was coupled with a profound connection to the heavens above. It was as if I was receiving divine support and encouragement from my Heavenly Mother who was right there with me, guiding and comforting me. The combination of physical exertion and spiritual presence created a powerful and transformative experience.

This was a day that changed the trajectory of my life. I met a version of myself that I wasn't aware existed. I experienced self-love and an immense appreciation for myself and my capabilities. It is still one of the hallmark moments of my life.

The entire process taught me that sometimes all it takes is one person to believe in you to help you realize your own capabilities. The nurse who believed in me played a crucial role, but more importantly, it was about connecting with a deeper part of me that knew I was capable of facing and overcoming incredible challenges. This wasn't just about proving something to others or myself; it was about tapping into a profound inner strength and resilience.

In those moments of pushing and birthing my child, I felt an intense mix of pain and empowerment. The pain was a testament to my strength, and the empowerment came from realizing that I could endure and triumph over the pain. Holding my baby in my arms was the ultimate reward, a tangible symbol of the strength and power I had discovered within myself.

This experience has left an undeniable mark on me. It has reminded me of the incredible potential and resilience that lies within us all. It has shown me that we are often stronger and more capable than we realize, and sometimes it takes a profound experience to uncover that strength. This realization continues to inspire and empower me in other areas of my life, reminding me that I have the inner resources to face and overcome any challenge.

To all the women out there, know that you, too, have an incredible well of inner strength. Life has a way of testing us, pushing us to our limits, and sometimes making us doubt our own capabilities. But within each of us lies a powerful force, a resilience that can carry us through the toughest of times. Trust in your own capabilities, for you are far more capable than you may think.

Surround yourself with those who believe in you and offer their support. Listen to the supportive voices around you, the ones who lift you up and encourage you to reach for your dreams. These voices can come from friends, family, or even those who have walked a similar path and share their stories. They can remind you of your strength when you need it the most.

Connect with that deeper part of yourself, the part that knows your true potential. This connection can be spiritual, emotional, or intuitive. It's about recognizing that you are not alone in your journey. Whether in childbirth or any other challenge life presents, believe in your power and resilience. Know that you have the ability to face and overcome incredible challenges no matter how insurmountable they may seem.

Sometimes, all it takes is a leap of faith and a little encouragement to unlock the strength within. Take that leap, trust yourself, and embrace the journey ahead. Remember that every step you take, no matter how small, is a testament to your courage and determination. Embrace your power, trust your journey, and know that you are stronger than you realize.

CHAPTER 32

EMBRACING OUR BEAUTY

Why can't we *be* our full beauty? Why are we afraid to be stunning as hell? Why do we downplay our success? These questions linger in the minds of many women, especially those who have faced the shackles of self-abandonment. Fear often drives us to hide our true selves, to downplay our achievements and potential. But this fear isn't just a personal battle—it's a societal one.

Fear of leaving abuse, fear of telling our story because it brings out hate in others who are silenced—these are real and powerful deterrents. The women who destroy us do so because of their own self-hate. They are angry at our liberation, angry at themselves for not being able to break free, and they take it out on us. We tell ourselves to stay shackled because breaking free would mean shattering the lies we have been fed and have believed for so long.

When one person leaves an abusive situation, it means the fears that kept them shackled no longer work. Those who leave crack the lie wide open: the lie that we are weak, that we are incapable, that we are nothing without our abusers. Your shackles are not locked. They never were. You have the power to leave, to embrace your full beauty and potential.

I left the pack, and they want to leave too. When we break free, we don't just liberate ourselves; we pave the way for others to follow. Our courage becomes a beacon, a light that others can follow out of their own darkness.

Abuse is a paradox. It makes us believe we are weak while simultaneously making us strong. Abused women are the least fragile women out there. There is nothing weak about someone going through abuse. It takes immense strength to endure, to survive, and eventually, to break free. Abuse makes us resilient, resourceful, and incredibly strong.

Abuse no longer holds us once we believe we are strong. This realization is the key to our freedom. When we internalize the belief that we are strong, capable, and worthy, the power of our abusers crumbles. Game over. The hold they had over us dissipates because their power was always rooted in our belief in our own weakness.

Telling our stories is a revolutionary act. It brings out hate in others who are still silenced, but it also brings out hope. When we share our experiences, we crack open the lie for others. We show them that it is possible to break free, that there is life beyond abuse, that they, too, can reclaim their power and beauty.

Embracing Our Beauty

The women who try to destroy us with their hate are still trapped in their own cages. They are angry at our liberation because it highlights their own chains. But our stories, our courage, and our strength can inspire them to find their own way out. We must not let their anger and hate silence us. We must speak our truths loudly and proudly.

In a powerful breathwork session, a drumbeat echoed in the depths of my consciousness, stirring a vision that transcended the physical realm. As I closed my eyes, I found myself enveloped in a scene that unfolded with vivid clarity. Standing in a flowing white dress, I noticed the muddy claw marks near its hem—a poignant reminder of the struggles and attempts to hold me back.

These muddy handprints were not just random marks; they were imprints left by those who sought to keep me tethered to misery. They were from the hands of individuals who couldn't bear to see me rise above their expectations, their own limitations, and perhaps their own insecurities. Each print told a story of resistance, of efforts to thwart my progress and keep me entangled in a web of doubt and despair.

Some of these handprints belonged to voices from my past—those who whispered words of doubt and inadequacy, planting seeds of fear and uncertainty in my mind. Others were the actions of people who couldn't bear to see me break free from the roles they had assigned to me, roles that confined me to their expectations rather than allowing me to embrace my true potential.

In the vision, these muddy claw marks stood out starkly against the purity of the white dress, symbolizing the contrast between oppression and liberation, between confinement and freedom. They marked moments when I had faltered, when I had almost succumbed to the weight of external expectations and self-doubt.

But as the drumbeat intensified, so did my resolve. The vision was not just about acknowledging these marks of resistance; it was about recognizing the strength within me to transcend them. Each muddy imprint became a testament to the challenges I had faced and overcome, a reminder that despite their efforts, I had persisted and prevailed.

In that moment of clarity, I understood that these handprints did not define me; they were merely traces of a past I was ready to leave behind. They represented moments when I had doubted myself, moments when I had allowed others' perceptions to cloud my own vision of what I could achieve.

The rhythm of the drum intensified, resonating through every fiber of my being. At that moment, I realized I was not alone. Surrounding me were millions of women all dressed in white, each bearing their own muddy marks of past trials and tribulations. Together, we formed a powerful assembly, united by a shared journey of overcoming adversity.

Looking down, we saw shackles encircling our ankles—symbols of the limitations imposed upon us by society, by others, and by our own fears. Yet, despite their appearance, there were no locks. The realization dawned upon us like a revelation: we had the power all along to break free. The shackles were merely illusions, upheld by our own beliefs and insecurities.

With a surge of collective empowerment, a wave of determination swept through us. It was a moment of clarity and defiance—a declaration that we would no longer be confined by the chains of doubt and oppression. As the drumbeat reached its crescendo, we made a choice together to step out of our shackles, to shed the weight of past pains and restrictions.

As we moved forward in unison, the chains fell away with a resounding *clank*, crashing to the ground like remnants of a bygone era. Each step we took was imbued with purpose and liberation. We were no longer bound by the narratives of weakness or victimhood. Instead, we embraced our strength, our resilience, and our inherent beauty.

In that vision of liberation, we found solidarity and empowerment. We recognized that our journey was not just about personal liberation but about paving the way for others to break free from their own constraints. It was a transformative experience, reinforcing the truth that true freedom begins within—within our minds, our hearts, and our collective consciousness.

Together, we walked forward, illuminated by the knowledge that we were capable of creating a future where women stand tall in their full beauty and power. The drumbeat continued to echo in our souls—a reminder of our unity, our strength, and our unwavering determination to embrace the boundless possibilities that awaited us.

As I stood in that flowing white dress, surrounded by the echoes of the drumbeat, I made a conscious decision to release the hold these muddy handprints had on me. They were no longer chains to bind me but reminders of my resilience and determination to forge my own path.

With each breath, I cleansed myself of their lingering influence, stepping forward with renewed purpose and clarity.

The vision became a transformative experience—a catalyst for embracing my full potential and shedding the layers of doubt and limitation that had held me back. It was a reminder that true liberation begins from within, from confronting and overcoming the barriers—both external and internal—that seek to confine us.

In this way, the muddy hand marks on my white dress became symbols of liberation—a testament to my journey of reclaiming my power, my voice, and my inherent worth. They showed me that even in moments of struggle and opposition, I had the strength to rise above, to embrace my true self unapologetically.

As I emerged from the breathwork session I carried with me a newfound sense of empowerment. The drumbeat continued to resonate within me, a steady rhythm guiding me forward on the path to self-discovery. With each step, I left behind the remnants of doubt and limitation, embracing the purity and strength symbolized by the flowing white dress.

Why can't we be our full beauty? We can. We must. Embracing our full beauty means acknowledging our strength, our resilience, and our worth. It means standing tall and proud, unafraid to shine. It means refusing to downplay our success or dim our light to make others comfortable.

We are stunning as hell. We have survived, thrived, and broken free from the chains that once held us. Our beauty is not just skin deep; it is rooted in our strength, our courage, and our resilience. We are beautiful because we are strong. We are beautiful because we are survivors. We are beautiful because we are free.

Throughout this book, we've explored the power of resilience, the importance of self-belief, and the necessity of embracing one's true self. These themes are not just words on a page; they are the essence of what it means to live a fulfilled and empowered life. As you turn the last page, carry these lessons with you. Let them infuse every decision you make, every relationship you nurture, and every challenge you face.

In closing, I want to leave you with this: the journey of self-discovery and empowerment is a lifelong one. It requires patience, perseverance, and a deep commitment to oneself. But it is also filled with profound joy, fulfillment, and a sense of purpose. As you continue on this journey, remember to celebrate your victories no matter how small. Each step you take is a testament to your strength and your unwavering spirit.

As we move forward, let us remember that we are part of a larger community of women who have faced similar struggles and triumphs. Share your experiences, lend your support, and lift each other up. In unity, we find even greater strength. By fostering a sense of sisterhood and solidarity, we can create a ripple effect of empowerment that reaches far beyond our individual lives.

Our stories, our voices, and our actions have the power to inspire future generations. Let us be the role models we wish we had, showing the

Rising: Fearless Women Rebelling

world that women can be both compassionate and formidable, nurturing and strong. Embrace the duality of your nature and use it to forge a path that is uniquely yours.

So let us rise, my sisters, and claim our rightful place in the world. Let us seize the opportunities that lie before us, and let us never settle for anything less than the extraordinary lives we were meant to live.

This is our time.
This is our moment.

Together, we are powerful.
Together, we are unstoppable.
Together, we will create a world where every woman feels empowered, valued, and unstoppable.
Together, we will shine, brighter than ever before.

Together we will RISE.

CHAPTER 33

YOUR TURN

It's time to begin writing your untold chapters. As you have reached the end of this book, remember that your story is just starting. Use the blank pages here to boldly inscribe your dreams, truths, and the powerful voice that is uniquely yours. When you're done, pass this book along to another woman, urging her to embrace her power and write her untold stories. Let this act be a torch, igniting a chain of empowerment from woman to woman as we all claim our strength and share our light with the world.

Your Turn

Rising*: Fearless Women Rebelling*

Your Turn

Rising*: Fearless Women Rebelling*

Your Turn

Rising: *Fearless Women Rebelling*

Your Turn

Rising: *Fearless Women Rebelling*

Your Turn

Made in the USA
Monee, IL
18 June 2025